SEVEN LESSONS FOR
DREAMERS & MAKERS

ILLUSTRATIONS BY MICHAEL MULLAN

ISBN: 978-0-578-73765-2
Printed in the United States of America

Illustrations by Michael Mullan
(M.F.A., illustration, 2010)

WHAT ONE CAN BE, ONE MUST BE!

−ABRAHAM MASLOW
Motivation and Personality

UP WE GO!

On April 26, 1336, nearly 700 years ago in what is now Southern France, at the western verge of the Alps, a wandering medieval poet named Petrarch stood at the foot of Mont Ventoux and did something remarkable: He climbed the mountain, because he could. Up until that point in history, mountaineering and indeed most exploration of any kind always had an adjacent purpose, ancillary to a military campaign, a religious pilgrimage, the pursuit of fortunes tucked away in some hidden crevasse. But not Petrarch. His ascent is the first in recorded history undertaken for the sheer delight and experience of it. He wanted the beauty, the view, the satisfaction and achievement. He wanted to live in a world where anyone could seek their own destinies and ascend to their own peaks.

In the seven centuries since, millions of others have followed in his footsteps up mountains both metaphorical and literal, from Junko Ishibashi (the first woman to summit Mount Everest—in 1975), to Kobe Bryant (the youngest player ever to start in an NBA basketball game—18 years old), to you. What do you want out of life? What peak do you want to claim as your own?

✳ ✳ ✳

As I write this, the world has only just begun to emerge from the strange fog of COVID-19, the largest public health crisis in a century. We will not fully understand the impact of the pandemic on human life and culture for many years, but one thing we do know: In the years ahead, young people will continue to dream, grow, learn, and long to make the world a better place, just as parents and teachers will continue to nurture students to discover their purpose and climb the great mountain of their highest hopes.

If you've studied psychology, chances are you've encountered the work of Abraham Maslow, the 20th-century American psychologist who wrote *Theory of Human Motivation* (1943). Maslow describes a "hierarchy of needs" every human has.

The theory goes like this—all members of the human race have basically the same needs: safety, food, love, shelter, community, and so on. But not all needs are created equal. Some are more essential, and only when we meet the most urgent needs can we ascend to higher stages of human development. For example, someone in dire need of finding food has little time to think about the long-term future or a career, just as someone without friends or family may never climb to the stage of self-esteem and self-respect. Thus, Maslow's hierarchy.

Uppermost in Maslow's pyramid is the stage of self-actualization, when each of us becomes who we were born to be. When parents, friends, teachers, and others encourage you to live up to your potential, that's Maslow's concept of self-actualization. They see something in you—a sign and premonition of success that you're fully capable of seizing with all your strength of mind and heart.

✳ ✳ ✳

MASLOW'S HIERARCHY of NEEDS

SELF ACTUALIZATION
ESTEEM
LOVE ♥ BELONGING
SAFETY
PHYSIOLOGICAL

Over the last century, Maslow's pyramid has revolutionized education, health care, social work, therapy, and just about every other realm of human endeavor. Previous generations believed that some were doomed to failure while others were predestined for success, whereas Maslow posited that *each and every human being holds within them the capacity to reach the peak of their potential.* If this idea—that each of us holds within us the capacity for greatness—sounds obvious in today's culture of self-care, thank Dr. Maslow, the O.G. motivational speaker.

In my long career as a teacher, academic dean, provost, and university founder and president, I've seen self-actualization happen again and again—that wondrous, chill-bumps moment when students discover who they are and what they were born to do. I've seen this miracle in labs and ateliers, on soundstages and sets, at fashion shows, jewelry exhibitions, showcases, readings, screenings, and company headquarters. I've seen nearly 50,000 university graduates walk across stages, graduates who are now working at BMW, Apple, Deloitte, and hundreds more top companies and startups and studios the world over, with clients in cities from Berlin to Beijing, Baton Rouge to Buenos Aires. I've seen what happens when you help young people discover a calling.

This book provides a path toward that triumphant moment of discovery, equipping students (and their families and educators) with actionable steps toward rewarding professions—for you and others in your life. We have distilled all our learning and research into these seven lessons, drawing on insights from SCAD alumni, professors, celebrated guests, researchers, and others who have learned and lived out these lessons in their own careers. Think of this book as a favorite teacher or professor, encouraging you with a little of their own wisdom. Our message to you, in these pages, is that every student has the power to articulate unique passions and translate those talents into a lifelong profession—that each of us can climb Maslow's mountain and become our best, most authentic selves. By the way ... the windswept peak of Mont Ventoux I mentioned earlier? It's visible from SCAD Lacoste, the university's European campus, where SCAD students from around the world travel every quarter to study.

Two caveats, quickly. First, though SCAD is a university for creative professions, this book is written for every student, no matter where those students are studying or hope to go. Future neurologists, pilots, attorneys, and veterinarians—this book is for you, too! What has worked for our graduates works for everyone who wants to learn, do more, and go further.

Second, I want you to take a deep breath and say it with me: There are no wrong career decisions. Choices lead to more choices. If you're anxious about attending the "wrong" college, remember: you can transfer. If you're worried that you might be in the "wrong" major, redeclare! If you fear you've chosen the "wrong" career, you can reenroll and earn another degree. It's not possible to have too much education. Your path will change. That's part of the fun. One of our graduates, Danielle, a successful designer with Catherine Macfee Interior Design in the Bay Area, changed majors four times. Another of our alumni, Chris, also a four-time major-changer, is now thriving as a user-experience (or "UX") designer with FireEye, a cybersecurity company.[1]

Again, no moves are wrong moves when it comes to your education. Every choice yields new discovery. What I love about Maslow's Hierarchy of Needs is how every experience equips you to ascend higher. Use those discoveries, keep them close to your heart, and get ready to climb. Up we go!

— Paula Wallace
President and Founder, SCAD

QUESTION EVERYTHING. EVERY STRIPE, EVERY STAR, EVERY WORD SPOKEN. EVERYTHING.

— ERNEST GAINES, *The Sky Is Gray*

HOLD YOUR HAND
HIGH

Few scenes fill a teacher with as much joy as surveying eager students with hands raised, ready to answer a question—from first-year students, bright-eyed and ready to take on the world, to grad students in architecture preparing for licensure exams. Student enthusiasm is a beautiful thing to behold, and every quarter, many of the world's best brands visit our university to tap into this fearless sense of discovery.[2] These companies partner with our students to investigate real-life questions about what's next in business and culture—such as:

> "How can we better serve elderly drivers?" (BMW)

> "What does the drive-thru of the future look like?" (Chick-fil-A)

> "What more can we do to help civilians in a natural disaster?" (Google)

> "Why don't Millennials like to grill out as much as their parents do?" (Char-Broil)

Keep in mind that these questions do not represent hypothetical student projects but rather real and professional research assignments with a bearing on each of these company's bottom lines.

These are questions these blue-chip companies brought to SCAD students at SCADpro, our in-house research and design consultancy.

Clayco, one of the nation's largest design-and-construction companies, recently came to our students with this question: How can we design a safer hard hat?

The assignment included SCAD students from five countries (China, India, France, Taiwan, and the U.S.) and four different academic majors (design management, equestrian studies, industrial design, and graphic design). During the first meeting, when Clayco executives posed the question, hands shot up all over the room. The students poked and prodded every assumption. They wanted to know: What causes jobsite accidents? Does everybody have to wear a hard hat? Are the hats all the same? How do users feel about wearing hard hats? How have hard hats evolved? When were they invented? Are they customizable?

Soon, students left the classroom and toured jobsites. They surveyed workers, read data, and performed field tests, which led to a remarkable discovery: The team learned that 90 percent of jobsite head injuries occur due to construction workers not actually wearing their hard hats—because, frankly, most hard hats are uncomfortable and hot. In other words, the question wasn't

"How can we design a safer hard hat?" but rather "How can we build a hat that people actually want to wear?" And then, after prototyping and more testing, they designed three.

Clayco has already moved students' designs into production, including the Captain, the Pollux, and the Jupiter. These new hard hats stand to save lives and resources—all because SCAD students asked questions and conjured smart answers.[3]

★ WHY HUMANS SUCCEED ★

The consensus in social science is that the two most important predictors of academic and professional success are intelligence and conscientiousness. Statistically, smart people who work hard experience the most success—no surprise there.[4] Yet, in a paper published in *Perspectives on Psychological Science*, researchers persuasively establish a "third pillar" of success, exhibited by every student who has ever raised a hand in class: curiosity.[5]

We at SCAD go one step further and say that curiosity is the single most important quality for any student to possess, because this quality bids us know *more*—to go further, ask, search, take risks. Study after study shows that an innate desire to learn (called "motivational giftedness") is a far more effective predictor of career success than I.Q., or intellectual giftedness.[6] All makers and dreamers are deeply curious, throwing themselves daily into the fray of discovery. They read fiction, nonfiction, newspapers. They consume podcasts like a major food group. They attend lectures and panels and exhibitions. They listen. They journal. They ask.

Persons who are motivationally gifted enjoy the process of learning as much as knowing—and are more comfortable asking questions and exposing the limitations of their knowledge. James Kennedy, an Australian chemistry professor, conducted an armchair study of his own students' curiosity, demonstrating with an unusually high correlation that those who had asked him the most questions via email were far and away the highest-achieving students in his class.[7]

Curiosity isn't merely about asking questions, though. Inquisitiveness is a state of being that compels dynamism: The truly curious are always moving, experimenting, reading, learning new languages, exploring new wellness routines. The curious build, draw, write, sing, perform, and throw themselves into new experiences, just to see what happens.

WHAT HAPPENS IS, YOU GROW

Pablo Casals, one of the 20th century's greatest cellists, practiced his scales every single day, well into his nineties. Practice: a ritualized process of discovery. (Call it "embodied" curiosity.) Most

young piano prodigies look at scales like a hazard to be overcome so that one might get to the good stuff, symphonies and suites and the Vienna State Opera. Not Casals. He coveted daily ritual.

"Why do you still practice for six hours every day?" baffled journalists asked Casals, every time they visited his home in Puerto Rico. Keep in mind, Casals had spent a lifetime recording and performing Bach, Brahms, Beethoven, Schumann, Dvorak, Mendelssohn, building one of the most impressive legacies of sound recording in the history of music. Here was the cellist who founded the Ecole Normale de Musique in Paris decades before! And still, he practiced every day. Why?

"Because every day, I learn something new," Casals said.

Even after retirement from public performance, he sat near a window overlooking the Bahia de San Juan, attempting to discover new sounds, unexplored techniques—more beauty for his arpeggios and portamentos.

What might Casals' curiosity look like in a college student? How enthusiastic are you about engaging in the most rudimentary rituals and necessary devotions of your chosen profession? If you want to study civil rights law or architectural history, how willing are you to devote hours weekly, daily, to reading and research? If you long to design products or cities, are you up for daily drawing in your Moleskine? If your dream is to write TV comedy, are you willing to spend an hour every morning studying the scripts of *Fleabag* and *Veep*?

///////////

CURIOSITY IS A HABIT OF HOPE

The life of Misty Copeland speaks to a very different brand of embodied curiosity. Copeland was born in Kansas City, Missouri, in 1982, the fourth of six children in a broken home. The odds were not in her favor, especially when financial difficulty carried her and her siblings from the Midwest to San Pedro, California, far from family and friends. By middle school, Copeland was quiet and withdrawn amid the chaos of life change.

"Looking back, I was so shy," she told *ELLE*. "I was miserable in school, because I was just like, 'I want to hide, and I don't want to talk'."

Copeland especially feared being called on by the teacher and was not one to volunteer to answer questions and march up to the board.[8] Yet at home she felt the urge to dance. Her body was capable of impressive flexibility. With no way to pay for dance classes, Copeland's only option was to join the middle school drill team.

"Have you ever taken ballet?" the drill team coach asked one day after practice.

Copeland had never studied ballet, never even seen a ballet performance, but the young teenager felt like something beckoned her to it. She found herself in her first classical ballet class on a basketball court at a local Boys and Girls Club.

Copeland felt like she didn't belong. Some of the other girls explained that they'd taken classes from age four or five, not in junior high. She felt out of place, surrounded by strangers, but something happened, once she finally summoned the courage to put hand to barre.

"It was the first time I ever felt beautiful," she said.[9]

She went back to the Boys and Girls Club for another class, then another, eventually seeking more and more intense instruction from her teacher, Cynthia Bradley. The young dancer soared from a makeshift studio on a basketball court to the San Pedro Ballet School and the San Francisco Ballet and, eventually, the American Ballet Theatre (ABT), where she was named to the corps de ballet in 2001, at the age of 18— a fairytale, considering she'd only taken her first class six years earlier.

Fourteen years later, at age 33, Copeland made history when she was named the ABT's principal dancer, the first African American female principal in the company's 75-year history.

Her story affirms the power of openness, that willingness to answer the call. At age 13, Copeland might have easily declined the offer to attend her first ballet class. Nobody would have held it against her. At every turn, she could have said no, that she wasn't ready, that she felt unprepared, but when the universe presented opportunity, she raised her hand and volunteered for the adventure, again and again, with curiosity and courage.

HOW TO CULTIVATE MORE OF BOTH

The lives of Casals and Copeland have much to teach about the virtues of continual learning and receptivity to opportunity. To nurture your own sense of discovery, you'd do well to heed those teachers, coaches, and mentors who suggest you try something new. If someone sees something special in you and recommends a particular major or course of study, that person is giving you hints about which doors you should bound through.

A study in *Cognition and Emotion* found that curiosity is highest in persons who aren't sure if they know the answer to a particular question. (Those with confidence in their answers exhibited the least curiosity of all![10]) So here's a suggestion: sometime during your first year of college, do something that would surprise your friends back home. Never been in a play? Find an audition. Not the sporting type? Join an intramural team. When you go home for break, make them scratch their heads. Old friends may scoff at first, but secretly, they'll be impressed, even envious. Freedom looks good on you.

CHANGE THE WORLD

Find opportunities to get out of the house—safely and responsibly, of course. A Pew study found that for all the glories of the internet, most curious people do their learning in physical environments—libraries, bookstores, museums, houses of worship—where discovery is built into the architecture.[11] Works of art and literature represent curiosity incarnate, illustrating the most enduring questions of the human condition. Now or very soon, go to places where those kinds of works live.

And finally, consider volunteering your time. Who doesn't want to change the world? It's no accident that those who give their energy to important causes also express more affinity for learning than those who don't volunteer. Raising your hand isn't just about answering questions: It's about answering the call of responsibility, too. The openness required to seek new knowledge also helps us see need where others don't. Look at the example set by President Jimmy Carter and First Lady Rosalynn Carter, who volunteer their time through Habitat for Humanity. The Carters have helped build thousands of homes—perhaps one reason for their long and productive lives. A study in *The International Journal of Voluntary and Nonprofit Organizations* found that charitable giving has a positive benefit to overall health and wellness.[12]

If you're going to find and flourish in your chosen profession, you'll need all the curiosity you can summon. Your journey will raise many questions. The more prepared you are to ask and answer, the better off you'll be. Those who move through their lives with hands raised are always better for it.

///////////

JOURNEYS ARE THE MIDWIVES OF THOUGHT.

— ALAIN DE BOTTON   The Art of Travel

NEVER MISS A FIELD TRIP

Of the many changes wrought to human life in 2020, the loss of mobility was felt by all—downtown streets oddly free of traffic, fewer planes in the sky, trains empty of commuters. While this change appears to have been an unexpected boon for air quality, one cannot deny the disappointment felt by the rescheduled research trips, postponed vacations, and canceled study-abroad programs. Even shorter excursions in our own communities felt different. For many of us, travel—as a distinct and essential part of the human experience—quickly became a distant memory.

This sudden change for all awakened a deep universal desire to experience the joy and wonder of travel once again. What is it about venturing somewhere new that stirs the human spirit so? One study recently found that travel experiences correlate to fascinating outcomes, including:

Increased curiosity (See: Lesson One)

More confidence (*You* try hailing a cab in a foreign language.)

A greater sense of fashion and style (When in Rome ... you see how they dress.)

The same study also found that engaging in international and domestic travel simultaneously increases students' desire for more education *and* students' attractiveness to college admission officers, because universities love curious, confident applicants.[13]

It is no secret that college professors enjoy teaching students with significant travel experience, as those students are generally more self-motivated and willing to explore new ideas. In a radically transformed world like the one we lived through in 2020—even when many of us remained safely at home for months or longer—the beauty and benefits of travel persisted. One needn't pack a passport to experience that magic.

COME FOR THE WELLNESS, STAY FOR THE NEURONS

Neurologists have shown that even brief travel experiences require the brain to expand its neural network, producing new dendrites (the fibers that connect nerve cells), largely by exposing the mind to unfamiliar environments. Relatively pedestrian trips, such as navigating a new grocery store or asking a stranger for directions, wake up the mind in ways that established routines don't.

When you venture somewhere new, you bring home a larger, more complex brain. Note, too, that the concept of "travel" is a much broader and simpler concept than most of us first imagine. The word itself might conjure steamer trunks and high-speed rail, but even a leisurely Sunday picnic has gifts to offer: increases in learning, serotonin, creativity, and wellness are all linked to short trips, especially time spent in nature. One thing is sure: challenges both global and personal can surely give us appreciation for the timeless pleasures of an hour or two under the shade of a tree with the soundtrack of birdsong.

A study by design firm Arup reports that the privilege of walking to work, compared to a long commute, increases someone's happiness "as much as if they'd fallen in love."[14] While many of us spent the better part of 2020 studying and working from home, the frequency of neighborhood strolls and recreational biking skyrocketed during the lockdown. We know that hiking, walking, and other ambulatory travel are proven to be as effective as antidepressants in combatting anxiety and depression. There's a reason the great thinkers of civilization loved to walk!

From Aristotle to Walt Whitman, artists, writers, and thinkers have long extolled the restorative power of nature. "Ecotherapy" improves eye health, mental health, sleep and longevity, and exercise.[15] As writer Anne Lamott wisely put it, "Almost everything will work again if you unplug it for a few minutes, including you." One need not journey to Spain and walk the pilgrim road of the Camino de Santiago to enjoy the benefits of a brisk constitutional.

• • • LIKE TRON, BUT BETTER • • •

Recent studies show that the health benefits of travel—e.g., fewer heart attacks and lower blood pressure (as a result of a reprieve from everyday normal stressors, such as dealing with difficult classmates and colleagues)—exist whether the journey is experienced physically or virtually.[16] At SCAD, architectural history professors have guided students on virtual tours of Thomas Jefferson's Monticello and Frank Lloyd Wright's Fallingwater. Painting and fashion professors have taken students on digital tours of the SCAD Museum of Art and SCAD FASH Museum of Fashion + Film. Art history students have explored Roman ruins across the South of France, including the Via Domitia, Pont Julien, and Pont du Gard. Remarkably, research has shown that when asked to retain their experiences, those who traverse virtual spaces have better recall of events and objects than those who experienced the same journey in the physical world![17]

Virtual reality (VR) technologies have already amplified and heightened the virtual traveling experience—whether for work, study, or fun. Architects now utilize VR tools for walkthroughs of construction sites, especially convenient when clients and designers are working remotely and spread out across the globe. In fact, the use of VR in architecture and design has become so common, that SCAD integrated VR tools into our architecture and building arts curriculum.

VR also offers solutions to "over-tourism" in popular locales, separating the experience from the impact of conventional tourism. "In some cases, this separation may be a good thing," observes travel writer Leslie Wu, "especially when it comes to illustrious destinations such as Venice that are literally sinking under the weight of unsustainable levels of tourism and the resulting environmental impact."[18] VR tours of Stonehenge, Machu Picchu, and even interstellar space are among the places any of us can visit, thanks to VR technology.[19] Jiachen Mo, writing at GlobalEDGE, designates virtual travel as the future of virtual reality—even utilizing the term "digital teleportation" to describe the end goal for many developers.[20] From classroom teaching to virtual business travel, VR will profoundly alter both the expectations and experiences of travel.

TRAVEL TAKES YOU TO THE EDGE

A few years ago, Shankar Vedantam, host of the *Hidden Brain* podcast, explored what's called the "Edge Effect," an ecological term describing "the point in which two ecosystems meet, like the forest and the savanna." This liminal boundary is where new

life forms flourish. Researchers have studied this same principle in human interaction, treating different cultures as distinct ecosystems, revealing that deep immersion in another culture significantly improves creativity.[21]

In the podcast, Vedantam speaks about a fascinating study on runway collections presented over 21 seasons in New York, Paris, Milan, and London. The study found that creative directors who'd spent the most time working abroad demonstrated a higher degree of creative innovation, as measured by industry buyers in the French trade magazine *Journal du Textile*. This observation inspired researchers to posit "the foreign experience model of creative innovations."[22] The deeper your engagement with another culture, the deeper your creative innovations become.

We've observed this same effect in the lives and careers of SCAD graduates, such as figurative artist Melinda, an American now living in Italy in the village of Sant'Arsenio near the Cilento Coast, a breathtaking stretch of the deepest blue water.

"My intention was to live in Salerno for only a few months," Melinda said. "That was five years ago."

● ● ● ● ● ●

Today, Melinda is fluent in Italian and has an impressive list of international clients and exhibitions from Barcelona to New York—an accomplishment she credits to her sojourn from Savannah to Salerno.

"Travel taught me to see with new eyes," she said. "When I first arrived in Italy, I took walks and wondered why all the doors in Salerno were painted green. I asked a local. He said they'd never even noticed."

Looking at Melinda's work is a bit like studying a map: In her *l'immigrata* series, you'll see poppies, native to much of Europe, married to Georgia marshes under those perennial gray skies the Dutch Masters so loved—the Edge Effect in full force.

TRAVEL EXPERIENCE REQUIRED

Every dreamer should know that travel experiences stand to benefit your future career, second only to specific job-related experience.[23] A related survey in the U.K. found that an astonishing 82% of employers believe you're a top candidate if you have travel experience.[24] Why? One study found that recent college graduates with travel experiences (e.g., study abroad) were more attractive, in part, because they're perceived to be more entrepreneurial and independent, requiring less supervision than other applicants.[25] Another study found that international travel enhances the employability of graduates due to increased skill in networking, experiential learning, and other soft skills required of most 21st-century work.

By the time she'd completed her interior design degree, Paula already had serious international travel experience. As a recent story in *Expat Living* explains, "With an Irish-American father and a Japanese mother, Paula grew up as a third-culture kid, living all over the world: Spain, Japan, California, Brazil, Scotland, and England."

In the 1990s, Paula had her heart set on working for Hirsch Bedner Associates (HBA), a major international interior design firm famous for its hospitality design. Recent projects include the Four Seasons Guangzhou, Park Hyatt Suzhou, and The One & Only Portonovi, Montenegro. Paula had seen the firm's work in a magazine and pinned it to her vision board. This was her dream: designing hotels around the world.

"She cold-called the HBA office in San Francisco," writes Melinda Murphy in *Expat Living*,[26] bluffing her way into an interview, even though she knew nobody with the company and HBA had not even seen her portfolio yet. She flew cross-country from Savannah to San Francisco and shared her passion for the company.

> **"You don't even have to pay me," she told her interviewer. "Just give me a desk."**

Within months, she was hired, not just for her moxie and M.F.A. degree in interior design, but also for her cultural and travel experience. Today, when most large companies have a multinational presence, employers want hires that look just like Paula—fresh talent who can engage international clients and colleagues, virtually and in person, without batting an eye. Paula proved a great hire—she's been with HBA now for 22 years and has led design work on Waldorf Astoria Shanghai, Four Seasons Singapore, The Westin Jakarta, and others. She currently lives in Singapore with her husband and two daughters, and is a partner in HBA's office there.

UNEXPECTED GIFTS

Perhaps the greatest gifts of travel are those moments of unexpected discovery afforded by those who dare cross oceans and continents to find what they hadn't even been searching for.

Tiffani was 6 years old when she announced to her family that she would one day live and work in Paris. Nearly 30 years later, after earning her B.F.A. in painting and M.A. in art history (and after opening her own gallery and developing an international client list), Tiffani spent the summer in the Alumni Atelier residency at our university's campus in Lacoste, France. One afternoon, as she was painting in her studio, the windows thrown open to the legendary light of the Luberon—the same light that gave us Cezanne and Van Gogh—an unexpected visitor appeared in the doorway: Pierre Cardin, one of the world's most iconic designers and entrepreneurs. Cardin bought several of her paintings on the spot and became her patron, which resulted in Tiffani's lifelong dream coming true: an apartment in the 6th arrondissement of Paris overlooking the Jardin du Luxembourg. Today, Tiffani splits her time between the U.S. and France.

In all of Tiffani's journeys, she hadn't set out across nations and oceans expecting to meet these career-making moments—because that's the beauty of travel, the luxury of discovery afforded by its vast, inherent unpredictability.

Even if you're too busy with life and school and family to get to Addis Ababa or the South of France, you can find beauty and surprise in shorter excursions. If you live in a city with a historic district, grab a coffee to go and spend an hour walking where you've never walked before. If you live in a rural area, make a new playlist and take a Sunday drive through the country, turning down roads you've never explored. Select a new route and a new destination, a state park, an overlook, somewhere curious and strange. Even reading a book on a park bench for a few minutes rejuvenates mind and body. Travel needn't be epic—but we highly recommend crossing continents and oceans, too, when next you have the opportunity.

Every day has the potential to awaken the spirit and expand the imagination. Accept the invitation, and you'll find yourself healthier, happier, more creative, and more prepared to succeed in your chosen profession. Go. See. Read. Experience. Welcome the new and different into your life. Serendipity reigns. Discovery awaits.

THE WORLD AWAITS

FRIENDS ARE MY ESTATE.

— EMILY DICKINSON, *in a letter to Samuel Bowles*

CAST YOUR DREAM CREW

When Christopher arrived at university, he possessed everything necessary to make his professional dreams come true—almost.

Scholarship? Check.

Career plan? Yep.

Friends? Not quite.

Christopher was far from his home in Baton Rouge, Louisiana, and knew nobody else at first-year orientation. His passions had seemed more like solo endeavors. As a boy, his first love had been sequential art, his free time spent reading comics, writing stories, and drawing Superman and other favorite Justice League superheroes.

"One day in fourth grade, I was drawing a comic and my friend asked me why my characters were all wearing the same thing," Christopher told *The Manor*. "I started sketching different outfits for them and became immediately obsessed with that."[27]

Christopher had discovered his destiny: clothes. In time, that vision became sharper in his mind's eye. He'd earn a degree, launch a label, show at New York Fashion Week, make it all happen.

On the surface, fashion might seem a relatively solitary endeavor (long lonely nights in the studio, sketching, cutting, sewing), and yet, by his junior year, Christopher saw the importance of building a strong group of friends—a squad to lean on, to call on, to give balance to the demands of the study of fashion design at a high level. One of those friends was Alexandra from Edgewater, Maryland, another fashion major he'd met in the halls and studios of Eckburg Hall, where they took most of their classes.

Alexandra then introduced Christopher to David, a screenwriting student from Sunrise, Florida, and they made fast friends.

"I loved asking David what he thought about colors and looks," Christopher said. "He had such a different perspective from the fashion crowd."

A few blocks north of Eckburg sits Morris Hall, where Christina—an aspiring marketer from Lexington, Kentucky—had begun researching her senior thesis. Christina wanted to create a business plan for a startup and had heard about the hotshot designer about to graduate.

"I was about to launch my own label," Christopher said. "I needed a business plan, and here comes this gorgeous and smart marketing student who wanted to launch a business plan." It was kismet.

Four years later, Christopher, Alexandra, David, and Christina all work for the company they created together: the Christopher John Rogers (CJR) label, which staged its second NYFW runway show to breathless reviews from *Vogue*, *ELLE*, *Refinery29*, *Jezebel*, *Washington Post*, and others. Christopher and his crew have already dressed Lizzo and Michelle Obama, and in 2019, he won the prestigious CFDA/Vogue Fashion Fund, one of the world's largest fashion prizes ($400,000!) to help launch his label.

#SquadGoals achieved.

EVERYTHING'S BETTER TOGETHER

The rhetoric of "living the dream" often seems to privilege the individual over the group, and that's a problem. You are the hero of your story, it's true: You're Superman (or Wonder Woman, or Black Panther, take your pick), and like Christopher, you need a Justice League. It's been widely proven that young people who belong to strong peer communities are more successful in school and their careers. Having friends means a larger network: You learn about academic and professional opportunities, who's hiring, where the paid internships are, and which professors write the best reference letters.

A strong peer network also increases your sense of purpose and ability to seize unexpected opportunities. A study published in *Developmental Cognitive Neuroscience* found that the neural circuitry associated with prosocial behavior also controls healthy risk-taking. In other words, students with strong friendships are more likely to be entrepreneurial.[28] You'll need to take many measured risks to seize the life you want.

Building a crew also helps you complement your own talents and gifts. Christopher saw competencies in others that would help him be a better designer. He saw in Alexandra a gift for precision and detail (she now serves as studio manager and maker of more than half of each collection). In David, he observed confidence and friendliness (he now serves as the studio director and manager of relationships with vendors and contractors), and in Christina, naturally, he noted an eye for business (she leads marketing and branding efforts). Just as biodiversity strengthens ecosystems, so a diversity of personalities and competencies strengthens your team.

The beautiful alchemy of a collaborative crew is that, while you each bring your unique talents to the table, everyone gets better. A study by the National Bureau of Economic Research looked at fitness improvements among squadrons of U.S. Air Force cadets (about 30 cadets per squadron) across four years at the academy. They found that individual members derived their motivation from others within the squadron and that, in one sense, motivation became the shared truth of everyone in the group.[29]

Strong networks benefit health and wellness, too. According to one study, high school and college students scored higher in "loneliness" than every other demographic, including retirees— a situation likely aggravated by rising rates of anxiety and depression among members of Gen Z.[30] There's a silver lining here, though: Today's students, more than any previous generation in U.S. history, are more comfortable speaking about their own mental health. For scale, consider that 50 years ago, about 5% of young people reported mental health needs; that number has more than quintupled to 27%, as a result of reduced stigma associated with anxiety and depression.[31] Your university of choice will likely provide counseling support services to help students struggling with mental and emotional wellness, and you should take advantage of those resources—and remember that everything is better when experienced and shared with your people. You deserve a community who sees you, hears you, and champions you. But where do you find them?

HOW TO BUILD A DREAM TEAM

When it comes to finding your people, all colleges are not created equal. Specialized universities do make it easier to find friends, we think, for the simple reason that a lot of the sorting happens long before class even begins. Cadets at the U.S. Air Force Academy already have much in common (passion to serve, desire to lead), as do first-year students in a medical or law school. SCAD is a special-purpose university, so SCAD students naturally build networks.

Even though our catalog features a vast array of disciplines, from equestrian studies to immersive reality, a theme of inventive entrepreneurialism runs through every SCAD degree program, which means students already share much in common before they even meet one another. While we're on the subject of specialized vs. general universities, it's important to emphasize that SCAD is simultaneously a "specialized" and a comprehensive university. We have more than 100 student organizations, world class museums, international festivals (in film, television, animation, gaming, fashion, fine art, and more), and a seriously competitive intercollegiate athletics program with recent national championships in lacrosse, swimming, equestrian, bowling, golf, and other sports. SCAD is big. You don't miss out on anything.

Graduates of SCAD, even from vastly different majors, often end up working together when they leave—an uncommon occurrence among most grads from more general universities, due to the simple fact that these grads usually study vastly different subjects that don't overlap professionally. (Stick around for the story at the end of this lesson for more on that topic.)

Wherever you find yourself studying, start building your crew early. Eliza and Jack met on move-in day, before classes had even begun. Their respective roommates were dating at the time, so they found themselves sitting together during orientation. They quickly became friends and cultivated a collaborative network with one another and other new classmates.

"In your freshman year, you're in classes with people who are into very different things," Eliza said. "First year, you're meeting people you'd never meet when you're a junior or senior and in more advanced classes in your major. You need people whose interests are different from yours."

As a result of meeting so many students from different but related areas of study, Eliza found courage to experiment with new forms, learning techniques from classmates studying photography, fibers, and industrial design, among other areas. Jack ended up majoring in photography and helped Eliza document her work for critiques.

"Making friends in a dozen different majors was almost like getting a minor in those subjects," Eliza said.

Jack agrees. "I was friends with people from every major," he said. As a result, he became the go-to for photographing the work of everyone in his group—friends preparing senior collections, process books, websites, portfolios, anything and everything. If his friends needed an image, Jack had it covered. They trusted him.

By the time Eliza and Jack graduated, their erstwhile roommates had long since broken up, but their own relationship deepened. They were married last year and launched All Kinds Studio, an online retail site selling tableware and other home goods. Today, they are traveling the U.S. in a converted bus that doubles as an art studio, creating work inspired by the great American landscape. The collaboration continues.

SUCCESS BREEDS SUCCESS

Take a page from Eliza and Jack's story and look around your classes for talent. Recognize and honor the connections you share with those who seem different from you. If you're an aspiring director, listen up in your next literature class, and you might tune in to someone who should help with your script. If you've got an idea for a new app and need an appealing interface, look to see who's drawing stylized portrait sketches during the lecture. You may have found your graphic designer. If you've had success with a recent group assignment, keep a good thing going and reach out to your teammates the next time you're in need of a skill set you might not have. If you've developed trust with someone, then you're likely to find your next collaboration just as rewarding.

During a recent SCAD Savannah Film Festival, our university community had the pleasure of hosting Grammy-winning film composer Alan Silvestri, composer for films like *Back to the Future* and *Avengers: Endgame*, scoring a generation of cinematic memories. Throughout his career, Alan has completed an astonishing 23 films with Academy Award-winning director Bob Zemeckis. When speaking with students during a master class, he remarked on that long partnership.

"I think it's like any marriage," Silvestri said. "It's all about trust. The more trust you build, the better the work becomes."

By the way, if you're studying online or have already earned your undergraduate degree, consider building your network with a little digital diplomacy. Find and follow accounts near and far that interest you. If you've read a book or seen a short film you love, find the filmmaker and let them know. You'd be surprised by how many CEOs, celebrities, personalities, and other makers and dreamers check their own social. Get up in the DMs! This is how Canadian illustrator Derek Desierto met his hero, style influencer Eva Chen. Nearly two years later, when Chen landed a book deal for her first children's book, *A is for Awesome: 23 Iconic Women Who Changed the World*, she reconnected with Desierto, and they've since done four children's books together, with more on the way.

A FAMILY AND FRIENDS BUSINESS

Long before college, Ciaran knew the value of a strong team, as he'd grown up playing sports and came to university in the U.S. on a scholarship to play soccer. In the 1970s, his parents, Brian and Rosie, founded Orior, a bespoke furniture company in Newry, Ireland. Ciaran initially had no interest in the family business. He chose instead to study film.

In college, he became close with his soccer teammates, including Richard and Jordan, among others. He dreamed of completing his B.F.A. and becoming a professional athlete, but a family medical emergency changed his plans, and a year before graduation, Ciaran returned home to take over the family business and finish his degree online.[32]

"For 40 years, we've been bespoke custom makers," Ciaran said. "The main reason I came back to the family business is because I never wanted to see that end."

The company's furniture has always been handcrafted in Ireland, and Ciaran wanted to debut Orior for the U.S. market; for that move, he needed help—a team with a heart for design and a mind for business. He turned to former classmates and teammates in the U.S.

⟨ **"You can't do things alone," he said. "You have to collaborate. You have to source someone who knows how to do something better than you do."** ⟩

Ciaran, now serving as creative director of Orior, built his U.S. team almost entirely from his college network—adding no fewer than six former classmates, including Jean (head designer), Jordan (art director), Richard (sales director), Logann (director of operations), Tom (project manager), and Stephen (sales manager). This team of Super Friends has collaborated to stage a complete rebranding for Orior and the opening of a swoon-worthy showroom in Tribeca, since featured by Architectural Digest, Domino, Lonny, and others across the industry.

Most successful leaders, entrepreneurs, creatives, and other professionals are fortunate to work alongside a Justice League of heroes. Domino recently asked Ciaran: If he could begin his career anew, what would he want to be?

"Exactly what I am now," he said, "a colleague to family and friends creating beautiful products."[33]

Find your squad and build the dream together. Few, if any, do it alone.

PICK YOUR PERFECT SEAT

Recently, student Gabriel Bautista broke Twitter when he asked a simple question about riding the subway. You may have seen the post: "All my New Yorkers, which is the best seat?"

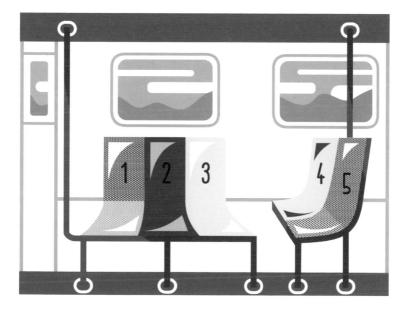

"A fiery debate soon erupted," according to the *New York Times*.[34] Some readers preferred No. 4, by the window, "tucked safely out of harm's way," while others chose No. 1, by the door, for a quick, clean exit.

"Definitely not the middle seat (No. 2), everyone agreed."

Others weighed in with a preference to stand, while some declared preferences based on height—Nos. 1, 2, and 3 being the only options, apparently, for the vertiginous.

Bautista's lighthearted query reveals a deeply human truth: We are passionate creatures, even when it comes to seating options, from subway and city bus (near the back, for peace and quiet) to restaurants (facing the door, obviously) and movie theaters (aisle seat, center row, with a buffer, natch).

Before college, many of your decisions are made for you by others: where you study, what you read, who your teachers are, how you dress (if uniforms are *de rigueur* at your school), even where you sit in class. Those limits largely vanish at university, where you now have remarkable freedom to choose your seat, as it were. Now comes the time to consider your gifts and talents. What do you love? What should you study? Perhaps you want to do it all: architecture, accessory design, writing, art history, social strategy and management, advertising, the list is endless—but time is not.

To echo a bit of useful wisdom in the prologue, there are no wrong moves in your education—including choosing your major. You'll carry the lessons of every course, every professor with you. Education is a universal good! The National Center for Education Statistics reports that nearly a third of college freshmen change majors at least once within three years of starting college.[35] For many students, switching a course of study is an important step in self-actualization. The more you learn about yourself, the more clarity you have about your passions. Now's the time to discover within yourself a calling, a passion, a course of study that invites your talents to flourish in beautiful and unexpected ways. You now have the freedom to pick the perfect seat. Which will you choose?

WIDEN THE ANGLE
— OF YOUR LENS —

In the 19th century, one's choices for university study rested rigidly within a catalog that included few options, typically Greek, Latin, mathematics, law, and natural philosophy (i.e., the hard sciences). In the early 20th century, degree options expanded, but only within the conventional categories of humanities and the sciences.

Gratefully, today's students live in a Cambrian explosion of academic choice. For example, students considering law, medicine, or engineering have far more career options today than even a generation ago. Students who excel in written and oral expression (a prerequisite for most law school applicants) now have the option to become writers for streaming series on Netflix, brand storytelling and marketing consultants, and UX designers for banking and tech firms—as did Laura, a native of Bogota, Colombia. Laura studied writing and service design and has applied her gift for storytelling to roles at Amazon and Bank of America, where she helps create more intuitive, inclusive digital experiences for clients and customers. Harrison employs his gift for narrative and storytelling in the $180 billion-a-year video game industry, where he works for Blizzard Entertainment, home of the *World of Warcraft* franchise.

Students drawn to STEM subjects and quantitative reasoning now have far more options, too. Erik had long been fascinated by automotive engineering, but rather than study the purely technical side of the industry, he chose to study industrial design. When he was still a college student, Erik and two of his classmates invented The Traverse—a full-size rolling concept car that was shown at the annual convention of the Industrial Designers Society of America.

That car caught the attention of aerospace company Bombardier, who flew Erik to Montreal for an interview and wasted no time in hiring him. A few years later, Erik accepted an offer from Honda, moved to California, and immediately started designing some of the baddest motorcycles in the business, like the Stateline Slammer—straight out of a Batman comic. Honda loved Erik's design so much they brought it to seven International Motorcycle Shows. In an alternate universe, Erik might have studied engineering, but thanks to increased opportunities for those with technical, analytical minds, he has built an unstoppable career with invention and style.

Companies and brands are desperate to hire social media analysts who know how to mine data and quantify strategies and results. Visual effects, motion media, and interactive design require a complex cluster of skills, including knowledge of coding. Industrial designers stand on the frontlines in the creation of the Internet of Things, marrying the efficiency of electrical engineering to the elegance of human-centered design. Students who love math and want to build should consider architecture, which demands intimate knowledge of calculus, applied physics, building materials, construction, fabrication, mechanical systems, and more.

Our university opened 42 years ago with eight majors and now offers more than 100 different degree programs. Widen your lens: See what's out there before you commit to something that doesn't capture your heart.

STOP, LOOK, AND LISTEN

Many students come to college with a major in mind, like Christopher, from the previous lesson, while many students wait until the end of their first year to declare. Both are fine options. You likely won't be taking any courses within your major until sophomore year at the earliest. But you should start exploring your interests more deeply, courting your passions, teasing them out of your personality. You have many professional possibilities living inside you, and they'll announce themselves in time. Your task right now is not to know absolutely everything about yourself, but simply to have an idea, an inkling, about who you might become, one day. The discovering is the fun.

As we've already discussed, your single greatest impediment to discovering your passion is simply a lack of knowledge about what courses of study exist for you to consider. While high school career fairs do help broaden vocational horizons, many young people end up settling for a career that feels familiar. A fascinating new report suggests that the jobs most likely to be passed on from parents include "steelworker, legislator, baker, lawyer, and doctor."[36] The data suggests that children choose their parents' vocation due to the "breakfast-table effect," where young people learn the rewards and challenges of these careers as a result of many conversations over time.

Most of us, one would guess, want to dream bigger than the breakfast table. How do you find out what college majors and careers are out there, available, possible? Your first resource is right there in your pocket. Take out your phone and request course catalogs (they're free) from a range of universities and colleges. Dogear the programs that speak to you. Mark up the tables of contents. Rip out the pages you love and plaster them on your wall for inspiration. While you're waiting on the catalogs to arrive in the mail (so retro), Google the phrase "best career aptitude tests" and take a few. Some take only five minutes. Think of these tests like a divining rod, hinting at where the wellspring of your passions might be found.

The purpose of these tools is to awaken the imagination and expand professional possibilities. Podcasts do this, too. Some of our faves include The School of Greatness (success stories from business and culture), Being Boss (for creative entrepreneurs), Women at Work (on gender and career), and On Creativity (part of the SCADcast suite of series, featuring conversations with some of today's top tastemakers and titans of creative industry).

If you're still floundering about your own course of study, why not reach out to some of your favorite high school teachers and coaches? These mentors often know you better than you know yourself. They've seen your work, your challenges, and your successes with their own eyes. Make a call. Send an email. Ask their advice. A recent Gallup survey revealed that a mere 11 percent of high school students seek guidance before choosing a college major.[37] Good advice is all around you, if you'll just ask.

ELF–ACTUALIZATION?

When Josh was a boy, he had a plan for his life, and that plan was to be an elf.

"I wanted to be Santa's Head Elf," he said. "It's true."

He grew up near the slopes in Vermont, so the possibility of a dream job in a winter wonderland was completely within the realm of possibility. And if you meet Josh, you can see it in his eyes, that unmistakable elfin gleam.

"It's the perfect job!" he said. "I wanted to be the guy with a clipboard, walking around, whistling while I worked, while everyone else whistled while they worked, making something that brings joy to the entire planet."

Josh grew up, as all children do, and forgot this wild arctic dream. At university, he chose to study digital media—broadcast design, specifically—and found himself drawn to collaborations with other classmates.

"I was the opposite of a lone wolf," Josh said. "I loved working on a team."

Making movies, he found, brought out the best in him and his friends. He devoted himself to collaborative work and sought out 24-hour film contests to enter with classmates, even while keeping up with his many demanding "official" assignments.

"We were having so much fun," Josh said. "And sometimes we even won—and made a little money. That made it even more fun."

By his senior year, Josh had changed his major to film and his specialization to producing. He and his friends built an entire production crew, ten students from across the university: industrial designers, actors, cinematographers, visual effects designers. They called themselves the Dandy Dwarves.

"We were magical people who made impossible things come to life!" he said.

After graduation, Josh produced films professionally—features, ads, short viral marketing films, you name it. He succeeded in this work so thoroughly, and with such joy, that SCAD eventually recruited Josh to return to his alma mater to lead a new creative initiative, one that would help students partner with the world's best companies to research and invent unique solutions to their business challenges. As you might imagine, producing films and producing results for clients require a similar skill set.

Today, Josh serves as the 'head elf,' as it were, of SCADpro, and it's not hyperbole to suggest that his work brings joy to the entire planet, given that he's leading collaborative assignments with Volvo, Uber, NASA—the list is long. He has helped Google reimagine Google Maps, oversaw production design for the 2022 FIFA World Cup, helped design concepts for Star Wars-themed hotels, and even led students in an assignment to create the Disney Princess Carriage for Dynacraft, now sold around the world. He's an elf, after all. Toys are his jam.

Josh's childhood daydream was all about inventing, creating, and building with a team of joyful makers, and he's found a way to turn that fantasy into an actual career. You can do the same. Think back to childhood. What did your dreaming heart long to be, when you grew up? The clues to your deepest passions are hidden in the answer to that question.

FIND YOUR QUESTION

Dreamers desire to make the world better, more beautiful, and more productive for everyone, and opportunities abound for invention. The world's far from perfect. There's work to be done. Look around: What needs fixing? What opportunities exist—in your life, your community—that need to be addressed? You might discover your destiny in a problem that needs to be solved.

A few years ago, we had the honor of hosting a master class at SCADshow with the inimitable Reese Witherspoon. Her story perfectly illustrates the power of a question to reveal your calling.

In 2015, Reese had achieved every marker of Hollywood triumph: box office results (in the hundreds of millions), critical praise (an Academy Award for her performance in *Walk the Line*), and cult status (as the star of audience faves like *Legally Blonde* and *Election*). By the time she was 39, she'd reached the Mount Everest of her career, and she wanted more. For one, there weren't enough great scripts for women. Women's stories weren't being told—at least not by women. Frustrated, Reese turned her attention to another passion project and launched Draper James, a clothing line with retail locations across the U.S., drawing inspiration from strong women in her life, her mother, grandmothers, and others. (Fun fact: Soon after the label launched, Reese and Draper James partnered with SCADpro, asking our students to design the label's first collection for children, which sold in Draper James stores in 2017 and 2018.)

The year Draper James launched, Reese was featured in a *Vanity Fair* cover story along with Gwyneth Paltrow, Jessica Alba, Blake Lively, and Lauren Conrad: five female stars who'd recently launched their own new companies. The headline read "Hollywood's New Domestic Divas" and the cover image depicted all five women in eveningwear, holding objects associated with housewifery—an iron, a vacuum, etc. The cover, the headline, everything was wrong. Reese got fierce. She made calls. She reached out to friends, other filmmakers, her people.

According to *The Hollywood Reporter*, "She wondered: Where was George Clooney and his tequila? Or Mark Wahlberg and his burger joints?"

Her male counterparts, Witherspoon said, are allowed to be entrepreneurial, but not women. "How dare we be anything more than actresses?" she said. "We, as women, are expected to stay in our lane—that was the inference, and I had sleepless nights over it. I remember calling one of these other women going, 'What are we doing about this?'"[38]

In asking that question, Reese's new passion was born. She discovered that she had a calling to tell stories with women at the center. She would break the system, or make an end-run around it.

In the years since, Witherspoon has set the entertainment industry on fire with her production company *Hello Sunshine*, landing a historic deal with Apple TV that included *The Morning Show* with Jennifer Aniston and Steve Carrell (made for $240 million, the largest budget in the history of television) and bringing *Little Fires Everywhere* to Hulu, not to mention *Big Little Lies*, the Emmy-winning HBO drama Witherspoon produces with a cast featuring Meryl Streep, Laura Dern, and Nicole Kidman.

Witherspoon now oversees podcasts, TV shows, feature films, her own interview series, books, audiobooks, and more ideas coming every day—all of it created in answer to that question: What can be done about the representation of women in media and culture? Like Reese, if you can find your question, you've found your calling.

Be the hero. Be fierce. It's hard to be casual about something you're passionate about. Do the research. Look for clues living inside your childhood fantasies. Find a problem that fires you up and set about solving it. Answer the call. Make the world more beautiful in a way you alone were born to.

RESEARCH IS FORMALIZED CURIOSITY. IT IS POKING AND PRYING WITH A PURPOSE.

— ZORA NEALE HURSTON,
author of
Their Eyes Were Watching God

DO THE HOMEWORK

On the night of Sunday, February 24, 2019, when costume designer Ruth E. Carter held her Oscar high for all the world to see, she made more than history—she made the world stand and cheer. At the Dolby Theatre in Hollywood, longtime fans leapt to their feet in wild applause and shouted for joy. Ruth won! Wakanda forever!

Carter's historic win for her epic Afrofuturist costumes in *Black Panther* (2018) made hers a household name, never mind that she'd already lead an impressive 30-year career, including work on 14 films with the great Spike Lee. From *School Daze* (1989) to *Amistad* (1997) to *Selma* (2014), Carter has dazzled the eye and the mind with her gift for evoking character through costume. And yet, her concepts do not spring forth from the mind unbidden. Everything Carter makes emerges from diligent, comprehensive research. She brings a scholar's intelligence to the work, her office a library of encyclopedias, fabric samples, vintage periodicals, and look books.

How do you design the wardrobe for a world like Wakanda? Where do you start?

RESEARCH

"Everything begins with research," she said to a packed house at a 2019 event in Atlanta in a conversation on her body of work.

Carter has made a career going on deep dives to piece together the backstories of her characters. During her research to prepare for *Malcolm X* (1992), for which she earned her first Academy Award nomination, she reached out to archivists and historians around the U.S., asking for documents and materials that might shed light on his story, which eventually led her to the discovery of a trove of letters written by the activist during his incarceration. Likewise, when it came time to create costumes for *Black Panther*, Carter knew to ask questions—starting with those who'd grown up with the comics.

"First, I called my brother, a police officer in Massachusetts," she said. She knew a little of the Wakanda story, but it was her brother and his fellow officers who helped the story come alive for her. "Everybody who'd grown up with these stories, wow—they had passion. They were believers!"

Next, she dove into the library, utilizing what she calls her "Design Bible" of Wakanda, with comprehensive input from the Marvel team: biographical details, narratives, and sketches of each tribe and historical references from tribes and nations across the African continent.

"We created the whole world, not on the page, but in 3D," she said. "We did it with good, old-fashioned research. And a lot of trial and error."

In the previous lesson, we explored finding your passions—and strange as it may seem, many dreamers stop there, believing the journey all but finished. Indeed, discovering your calling can feel like you've arrived, or at least found a clear path to seeing your dream made real. But there's more work to do. Whether you've just begun looking at colleges or you're already contemplating graduate school, you have questions to ask of yourself and the other influencers in your orbit. You've got to follow Ruth E. Carter's lead and do the homework.

YOUR FIRST ASSIGNMENT
VOCATION OR AVOCATION?

Research need not begin in the library. First, look in the mirror and ask yourself: Which of your passions are worthy of becoming a vocation? The word itself, *vocation*, is rooted in the Latin *vocare*, or "to call." In other words, a vocation is the profession your deepest passions summon you toward. One's avocation, on the other hand, can be something as simple as a favorite leisure activity (e.g., gardening, running, tennis) or a more serious pursuit that exercises body and mind in a deeper way (e.g., playing viola in a community chamber orchestra, serving on the board of your local rescue shelter), requiring more time and devotion than a hobby.

Not every passion need be a profession. One can find district attorneys who dogsled and dentists who compete in dance competitions. President Barack Obama has written five books, including two literary memoirs—rare for a world leader. A few years ago, President George W. Bush shocked the world with *Portraits of Courage*, a book featuring his paintings of wounded veterans, outing himself as a gifted visual artist. Both former U.S. presidents knew their passions (statecraft, writing, painting) and yet made important distinctions between vocation and avocation.

Like Bush, actor Jim Carrey paints. Like Obama, punk legend Patti Smith writes. Actor Ellie Kemper (of *The Office* and *Unbreakable Kimmy Schmidt*) is a devoted triathlete, and if you happened to watch the 2020 Grammy Awards, you learned that Lizzo is a gifted flautist. Like these cultural personalities and millions of working professionals the world over, you likely possess many gifts—both a blessing and a challenge. Do a little homework on yourself and determine which gifts can power a career.

"You are wired to excel in very specific and powerful ways," Steve Olsher wrote recently in *Forbes*. To cultivate a rewarding life, he says, you'll need to look at everything you're good at and make some choices.

Make a list of what you love to do. Decide which could become a profession and which should remain an avocation, something that rejuvenates and enlivens you alongside your primary career. Our next assignment can help you do that.

YOUR SECOND ASSIGNMENT
►►GET NAMES◄◄

Once you've determined which of your passions to pursue professionally, it's time to explore industries that need your talent. Many students skip this question entirely, trusting that their professors will tell them where to apply for jobs when the time comes—or relying on the tired adage that anyone who desires

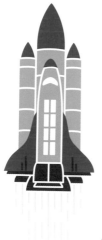

success is limited to becoming a doctor, lawyer, or engineer. Not so!

The next time you're on a college visit, meeting with a department chair, or interviewing for graduate admission, ask where their alumni work. Get the names of employers and actual job titles. If a university isn't prepared to provide those answers, they may not be best suited to prepare you for your professional future. Ideally, academic leaders should have copious information to provide on this subject—lists, names, and LinkedIn contact info, in case you want to dig deeper. While you're at it, ask about the acceptance rate for their alumni to graduate and professional schools.

If you ask where SCAD grads are working, you'll discover an entire world of professional possibility for every passion and predilection under the sun. You're just as likely to find our alumni working at places like Microsoft, Hewlett Packard, Lenovo, Ford, Porsche, Deloitte, Booz Allen Hamilton, McKinsey, Bank of America, Uber, NASA, the CDC, and the CIA as companies like Apple, NBC, Disney, and Pixar. We're known as The University for Creative Careers, and for good reason.

Once you learn *where* a program's graduates work, ask *how many* of the university's recent grads are working. This data point is a crucial benchmark for any institution that aims to prepare students for rewarding careers. According to the National Center for Education Statistics, in 2018, the national average employment rate for young adults with a bachelor's degree or higher was 86%. While some institutions don't report the employment rate for their graduates, many do. Ask! A university that publishes its employment number is a good sign—an indicator that the institution is proud of their graduates and proud of their results.[39]

YOUR THIRD ASSIGNMENT
· · · · · GET CREATIVE · · · · ·

As we shared in Lesson Four, today's students enjoy a multitude of career possibilities far beyond the staid categories of yesterday. There's an equally positive flipside to this vast expansion of modern professions: Just as those oriented towards STEM disciplines can find rewarding creative careers in everything from architecture

to automotive design, those who know they want to work in a creative profession can choose just about every industry under the sun, from finance and insurance to the mammoth economic sector of health care, all of which desperately need design talent.[40]

Every day around the world, designers and other creatives work to improve health care outcomes for patients.[41] Consider Shannon, who studied design management and now works as a senior design researcher for health care outcomes at 3M, employing her education to improve the lives of others.

Have you noticed how much easier it is to fill prescriptions these days, via your phone or online? Thank a service designer. Or maybe you can tell that waiting time at your family doctor's practice has seriously improved? Just a few years ago, you might have waited an hour for a checkup. Today, most patients wait hardly a few minutes, thanks to design leaders who have helped the health care industry become more efficient, compassionate, and patient-centered. Interior designers create more humane environments for healing, just as industrial designers create more patient-friendly medical devices.[42] Animators and immersive reality designers work in medicine, too. AR and VR solutions are already providing valuable resources for health care professionals, such as the virtual surgical training tool created by London Startup FundamentalVR.[43]

Assume nothing. When you're researching universities, ask educators what industries their grads are entering. If you love the economic opportunities of finance and the imaginative opportunities of design, you can satisfy both desires. Take Joel, an industrial design grad now serving as a senior vice president of design and innovation at Fifth Third Bank in Cincinnati, Ohio. Think more broadly about the industry your vocation might be calling you toward. You have more options than you know.

• • EXTRA CREDIT • •
1 2 3 GET NUMBERS 4 5 6

How can you be sure that you're getting the maximum return on your educational investment? During your next college tour, while you're vibing with the atmosphere, scoping out the dorms, and making notes, take time to go the extra mile and ask these additional questions many students never ask:

"May I see the results of your most recent accreditation?"

• • • • • •

Just as diners often check the official restaurant scores to get the scoop on an establishment's food-handling practices, students and families should reference a university's most recent accreditation results to learn about its operational health. Most universities hold multiple accreditations; some accreditations are required for specific disciplines and others cover the entire university. (The oldest, most important, and most rigorous form of accreditation is called *institutional accreditation*.) SCAD holds four different accreditations, including our regional accreditation—SACSCOC (Southern Association of Colleges and Schools Commission on Colleges)—as well as accreditations from NAAB (National Architectural Accrediting Board) and CIDA (Council for Interior Design Accreditation).

The delivery of accreditation results varies depending on the accrediting body, but, generally speaking, universities should be able to provide you with a report or determination letter that affords insights into curricula, student achievement, and more.[44] Be especially sure to read the section containing recommendations for improvement: If there are any weaknesses noted, ask what steps have been taken to ameliorate these deficiencies. You can also take the pulse of the institution by noting whether or not it has been awarded the maximum term of accreditation. Most people won't eat at restaurants that score less than an A+ on a health inspection, and that's for a single meal. Consider this distinction when choosing where you'll pursue your degree. It could lead to a better career.

"What percentage of students reenroll after their first year?"

•   •   •   •   •   •

In higher education, this number is referred to as "student retention" and is usually defined as the percentage of first-time, full-time undergraduate students who return to the university the following fall. Most universities do publish retention data on their website. Find out where and study the data. To put it simply, high retention means great students stay at great institutions. The national student retention average is currently 81%. Students and their families should only seriously consider universities that meet or exceed that number.

If you're looking at graduate schools, ask them about their thesis completion rate (i.e., the percentage of grad students who complete their master's degree requirements). This information is not collected nationally, but top universities track the data and should be able to provide it to you upon request. Anything less than 90% for thesis completion suggests that the university may not go far enough to help students complete their graduate requirements.

"What percentage of students graduate every year?"

• • • • • •

This number indicates a university's graduation rate, defined as the percentage of first-time undergraduate students who complete their program at the same institution within a specified period of time (usually four to six years). This information should also be viewable on a university's website. Administrators can tell you where to find it; a quick Google search works, too. According to the National Center for Education Statistics, the national graduation rate is currently 60% for first-time, full-time undergraduate students.[45] You should strongly consider universities that meet or exceed this rate.

"What is the student loan default rate for your graduates?"

• • • • • •

This data point, reported every year by the U.S. Department of Education, describes the percentage of a university's graduates who default on their student loans within a given cohort. For fiscal year 2016, for example, the national cohort default rate was 10.1%.

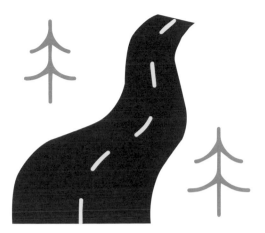

Loan default rates are like golf scores: lower is better. A university with a high default rate (i.e., anything higher than the average) may not be preparing their graduates for their professions, resulting in more of their alumni being underemployed, unemployed, and/or otherwise unable to pay back student loans. A healthy, low default rate is a positive indicator that a university prepares graduates for their professions.[46]

HOMEWORK NEVER REALLY ENDS

Scary, yes, but the reality is that no matter how many diplomas you frame, the rigors of independent research remain necessary throughout any career. Every academic and professional role in your life requires the diligence to ask tough questions of yourself and the institutions to which you're entrusting your education.

Just as Ruth E. Carter's long career in film has demonstrated, research powers the careers of every professional working at the top of their game. If there's a secret weapon to ascending Maslow's dreamy hierarchy, this is it right here: Ask the right questions. Get the answers. Go further and deeper—and let the facts inform your every move.

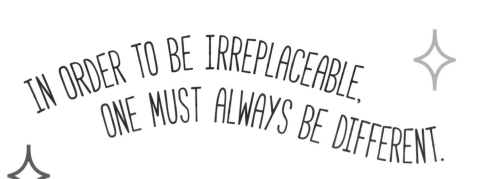

IN ORDER TO BE IRREPLACEABLE,
ONE MUST ALWAYS BE DIFFERENT.

— COCO CHANEL,
designer and founder of Chanel

BE THE ✏ UNICORN

As an undergraduate, Tabish studied computer science and found success working at startup labs in and around his home of Karachi, Pakistan. More and more, though, he found himself drawn as much to the aesthetics of digital environments as to the coding. Former classmates and colleagues, it seemed, were entirely focused on programming, and he spotted an opportunity to do what nobody else was doing.

"I had a visual sense, which was different," he said. "I had this talent, and I needed to do something about it. I needed a degree that would combine coding with creative."

He took a risk and left home, crossing the pond to study in the U.S., earning an M.A. in interactive design. Before he'd even finished his second degree, he'd found work with clients like Vans, Ford, and Microsoft—and landed a paid internship with Adobe, where he found his true calling, designing tools to make people more creative in their own lives. A few weeks before graduation, Google made him an offer.

"It was Google!" he said. "Who wouldn't want to work at Google?"

● ● ● ● ● ●

Following graduation, he moved to Mountain View, California. At the time, everybody was vying to work on Google Glass, but his first assignment took him to the YouTube Premium team, helping influencers make their videos more engaging. After a year, he received a call from Geoff, his former boss during his Adobe internship. Turns out, Geoff was also joining Google and wanted to invite Tabish to join his new Google team. Tabish was honored—and curious.

"What's the project?" Tabish asked.

"Hardware innovation," Geoff said. "Specifically, Google Glass."

Within a couple of years, Tabish was leading the New Wearable Technology team, which also included opportunities to work on Google's wireless earbuds, Pixel Buds.

Everybody, apparently, wanted to work with Tabish. Why?

Tabish is a unicorn—that professional with a rare combination of gifts few possess. Unicorns are the copywriters who also know InDesign, the data analysts who can create their own storyboards, the programmers and platform architects who understand the centrality of visual and aural design in providing users a more personalized experience. Tabish's rare combination of talents has equipped him to lead a team that features motion media designers, visual designers, interactive designers, and programmers.

"When I was at university, I wanted to learn everything I could. You're only there for a little while. You have to do it all! I took courses in animation, motion design, 3D, even though those weren't in my primary area of study," he said. "That opportunity, to learn things far beyond my main focus, is essential to my work today. I feel like I can just jump on anything, you know?"

SUPERHEROES KNOW A THING OR TWO

Wolverine doesn't merely have retractable claws: He possesses the ability to heal himself. The Hulk isn't just incredibly strong: He holds seven doctorates (seems excessive, but you get the idea). Even Squirrel Girl has more than one superpower—look her up: she's real!

Back here in the real world, we find a similar story. Our most talented SCAD grads (and the leading lights who visit the university and share their wisdom with our students) are invariably good at more than one thing. Almost always, they have some secret skill that elevates their work and proves invaluable to a team and a company. More often than not, these professionals double-majored at university or pursued a graduate degree that complements their undergraduate education, as Tabish did. Either option is the surest way to cement your status as a unicorn.

Ask any CEO or recruiters from the world's great companies, and you'll discover they desire team members who are skilled experts, not generalists. They hire contributors and leaders with

unique and highly specialized competencies. Your first 12+ years of education leading to college centers on general knowledge. Most people don't realize that the original seven liberal arts—grammar, logic, rhetoric, arithmetic, geometry, astronomy, and music—were originally intended, in the Middle Ages, as *preparatory* for university study toward a specific profession. Today, the principle remains: University is the time to specialize.

WHAT A DOUBLE MAJOR CAN DO

If you're anxious to get a jump on your career and want to bypass grad school (M.A. and M.F.A. degree programs typically take one, two, or three years), consider a double major. According to a study featured in *The Chronicle of Higher Education*, double-majoring has proven to increase integrative thinking, which "entails learning the deeper, underlying meaning of a discipline, making connections across courses and subjects, and applying different

intellectual perspectives."[47] Regardless of your area of study, from the hard sciences to the humanities, a second complementary major improves creativity and provides students with the ability to produce the most thoughtful, original, unexpected ideas. A study commissioned by the Teagle Foundation found that a double major helps one "think differently, solve intellectual puzzles, and approach assignments more creatively."[48]

Consider the "Edge Effect" from Lesson Two, which describes how those who spend time in other cultures and foreign countries exhibit significantly increased creativity. In many ways, a double major provides the same benefit, transporting you to a whole other country of the mind, so to speak. It's a bit like cross-training for athletes. Team doctors and other medical experts will tell you: Athletes benefit from playing multiple sports, working different muscle groups and adding variance to body and mind. Legendary Chicago Bears wide receiver Willie Gault took ballet classes to improve his balance and extension. Ballet provided Gault an added grace and power that made him one of the fastest players in the history of the NFL. Similarly, the study of design equipped Tabish with a fresh perspective most pure programmers don't have. He can speak more than one professional language.

Double majors, like those with advanced graduate degrees, also tend to find jobs more quickly and earn higher earnings than their single-major classmates.[49] A paper in *Education Economics* estimates that double majors earn 4% more than single majors, which over a lifetime, compounds into serious economic advantage. This income benefit holds across industries, from architecture to health care and entertainment.[50]

Maybe you're still not convinced. We've heard students say, "I really want to double major, but I don't have time! I want to finish and get to work!"

Others say, "I want to graduate with my friends."

Or, "My scholarship won't allow it."

Double majors generally do graduate on time. Most undergraduate degree programs require somewhere between 30 and 40 courses, and the Teagle study mentioned earlier found that double majors generally only take an average of three or four more courses than single majors—doable in a single summer. Better still, the majority of students report that double-majoring was not an impediment to social life or student activities; in fact, double majors report doing *more* social activities in college than their single-major counterparts.

As the saying goes, people who do more, do more.[51]

DEEP OR WIDE?

Most unicorns generally fall into two categories. "Deepeners" study two closely related subjects, delving deeply into a single discipline. Consider Zhu, who studied animation and motion media and now works for BMW North America, or Christopher B., who studied design for sustainability and industrial design and now works at Booz Allen Hamilton as a consultant. Two famous deepeners: Michael Eisner, legendary and longtime Disney CEO, who doubled in English and theater, and actor Denzel Washington, who studied drama and journalism.

"Wideners" like Tabish are more common, choosing two seemingly disparate subjects, as with Jordan, who studied writing and graphic design and merged both beautifully in her career as a book designer (she designed Oprah's latest bestseller, *The Path Made Clear*, among others). Alexandra H. is another widener, melding jewelry to fibers in her role as a designer for Tiffany & Co.

Two famous wideners: Susan Wojcicki, CEO of YouTube, who doubled in history and literature, and Elon Musk, who studied physics and economics. Mira Nair, the award-winning Indian director of *Monsoon Wedding* and *The Namesake*, studied sociology and film, and these two totally different disciplines are evident in her deeply ethnographic storytelling.

Here's a glance at a few more unicorns from our university and where they're working now (their double major areas of study are in boldface):

JASON **Computer Art & Illustration**
CREATIVE DIRECTOR, ACTIVISION BLIZZARD

Photography & Graphic Design COLIN
FOUNDER, SATURDAYS SURF NYC

CORRINE Interior Design & Fashion
DESIGNER, CHICK-FIL-A

Photography & Graphic Design **ERIN**
UX RESEARCHER, GOOGLE

ADRIANA Animation & Illustration
MULTIMEDIA SPECIALIST, NASA

Fashion & Accessory Design **KYLE**
FOOTWEAR DESIGNER, BANANA REPUBLIC

LINCOLN Service Design & Industrial Design
SERVICE DESIGNER, CITY OF AUSTIN, TEXAS

Design Management & Industrial Design **YUNMAN**
EXPERIENCE DESIGNER, YAHOO!

Do you want to dive into closely related subjects (psychology and neuroscience), or do you want to cast the net wide (studying visual effects and art history or business)? Open the catalog of your first-choice university. Circle every major you'd like to study. Which combos feel most promising? Which make the heart sing? Which pairs of majors will make you a lifelong unicorn?

WHAT HE'S DOING NOW

After six years at Google, Tabish has recently moved up the road a few miles to Facebook, where he now works on the New Product Experiments team. His unique cluster of talents, marrying his foundation in computer science to interactive design, has transformed him into a highly specialized unicorn every leader wants. His specialization has paid off because his network is now incredibly broad. Tabish's relationships now extend to the highest levels of the biggest companies in Silicon Valley. He's got friends and colleagues everywhere: Apple, Google, Facebook, Instagram.

"Silicon Valley's a small place," Tabish said. "You never know who you're going to work with next."

If you're earning a college degree (or about to) or preparing for grad school, now's the time to sharpen your secondary skills with a complementary discipline—enhancing your competencies to ensure varied opportunities and greater future earnings. This is the time when you should be learning as much as possible, immersing yourself in knowledge and experience. Never again in your life will you have such immediate access to so many experts and educators ready to share their wisdom! Take advantage. Double major. Minor. Stay on for a graduate degree. Give yourself more than one skill. Become the priceless unicorn you were born to be.

NOTHING SUCCEEDS LIKE SUCCESS.
GET A LITTLE SUCCESS,
AND THEN JUST GET A LITTLE MORE.

— MAYA ANGELOU,
author of I Know Why the Caged Bird Sings

TREAT EVERY DAY
▶ ▶ ▶ ◆ ◀ ◀ ◀
LIKE THE FIRST

After graduation, Lucas left his home in Springfield, Missouri, and followed his heart all the way to Los Angeles. His family encouraged him, like all good families do. He'd studied and performed musical theater, improv, and dance. He was ready for anything. He could see the fairytale unfolding before him—and it did, just like in *La La Land*, the auditioning, waiting, hoping, more auditioning, more waiting, more rejection.

"It was hard to make friends," Lucas said. "I was young. I didn't know many people."

Then one day, waiting in line for a smoothie, someone approached.

"You got a look, kid," the man said, like something from a movie. "I've been in the industry for thirty years. Have you ever thought about being an actor?"

"Yes," Lucas said, flashing that bighearted smile. "That's why I moved here!"

"Do you have a manager?" the man asked, pulling out a card.

Lucas couldn't believe it. Just like that, he had representation, someone to help him book the right auditions. Immediately, his new talent manager helped him get more callbacks, which meant—you guessed it—more waiting, more hoping. Lucas was especially interested in animation. He had an arsenal of cartoon voices, but nothing panned out.

"Things were not good," he said. "I had a manager, so I auditioned for a lot of voiceovers, but never got any jobs."

His life didn't feel like much of a fairytale, but Lucas kept smiling and auditioning, again and again—a dozen auditions, then a 100, then 200, with nothing to show. He worked hard not to be angry or bitter when roles went to others. He'd made a few friends. He was happy for them. He gave no thought to going home to Springfield. Instead, he got creative. He made a plan, bought a microphone, a new laptop, and turned his closet into a recording studio. He mixed and edited his own voice auditions and submitted his reel to every contact, every producer, every casting agent he met. He knew his fortunes would change if he'd stay with it.

AND THEN EVERYTHING CHANGED

In 2005, three years after his first professional audition, Lucas was cast in a small made-for-TV movie for the Disney Channel called *High School Musical* (HSM), which would go on to become one of the biggest sleeper hits in film history, earning hundreds of millions and giving Lucas Grabeel, in his role as Ryan Evans, the plot twist his own story needed.

"My world changed," Lucas said at SCAD in a recent podcast interview.[52] In addition to the three HSM movies and two international tours, Lucas finally launched the animation career he'd always wanted, too, landing roles in *Family Guy*, *The Cleveland Show*, *Robot Chicken*, and *Pinky Malinky*, his new series on Netflix, where he plays a talking hotdog in middle school. It's the stuff of dreams—or at least, his dreams.

It took Lucas 250 auditions to land that star-making role on *High School Musical*. So many young performers don't make it to a dozen auditions before becoming disheartened and walking away, defeated.

What's the secret? How'd he stay with it?

"You have to have that same fire in you from when you made that first decision that this is what you wanted to do with your life," he said. "Still, to this day, I go back to that moment, to that little kid who dreamed big. I get chills just thinking about it."

This is what our seventh and final lesson is all about: stoking the fires of hope throughout every season of your journey. Surely you recall the unbridled joy and wonder you felt on your first day of school, long ago, when you were younger—that sensation of endless possibility, new friends, fresh school supplies, a pristine backpack. The world was wide open, and anything was possible.

A study in the *Journal of Experimental Social Psychology* suggests that approaching your work with the mind of a beginner—even after you've become a seasoned expert—increases your ability to learn, grow skills, and activate more creative thinking. This mental habit is known as "open-minded cognition."[53] Lucas's career perfectly exemplifies this approach, this gift for remembering and rekindling the fires of optimism and enthusiasm he felt at the advent of his professional journey. You can nurture that gift in yourself, too. All it takes is the courage to remember. Treat every day like a new gift. You might make 249 attempts before that 250th audition (or interview, or pitch, or revision) lands you the job of a lifetime.

SUCCESS REWARDS A PLAN

One way to keep smiling, even amid the hardship and rejection that come with any big dream, is to focus on, and plan for, your successes—and not your failures. This advice may seem obvious, but no: In the wider culture, mad choruses of voices goad us to plan for failure. Commencement speakers, motivational coaches, and op-ed writers appear enthralled with glorification of the "F" word. Google "failure" right now, and you'll find countless blogs and videos of speeches on the many virtues of what, for most of human history, has been considered a bad thing.

"Failure is good!" they tell us. "Just keep failing, and you, too, will succeed!"

All this bluster of "Failure-ism" has the ring of authenticity and counterintuitive wisdom. It can be thrilling to hear the most accomplished persons in our society share heartbreaking stories of professional disaster. There's just one problem: Failure-ism doesn't work! The Centre for European Economic Research, for example, has found that entrepreneurs who had previously failed were no more likely than novices to launch a successful venture.[54]

At the heart of this perspective lurks an unproven, almost romantic notion of the value of randomness. What so many motivational speakers seem to be saying is that if we just open ourselves to the possibility of failure, then something positive will happen, as if by sorcery. There's another educational term for unhinged freedom and playfulness: it's called "recess." Play has a place in school and life, absolutely, but in your own pursuit of professional success, you'll do better to clearly define expectations and crisp benchmarks. In many ways, this book has been designed to highlight that central truth. Success requires research, planning, and action. Randomness has no quarter here!

The best English teachers, for example, don't merely ask students to "experiment with" or "try" writing a poem—an educator who wants students to succeed will explicate the actual steps of composing a sonnet, from ideation to drafting to revision to final recitation for the class. A great golf coach doesn't hand you the club and tell you where to hit it. A great coach models and teaches the discrete protocols of a swing: stance, grip, position of the head and shoulders, angle of body. Every step must be rehearsed and executed with intention. Success at each benchmark creates positive reinforcement for success at the next benchmark.

Lucas had a plan. He didn't merely get to Hollywood and wait for it to happen. He transformed his closet into a studio and created a demo reel and a website to showcase his talent, breaking down his Big Dream into clear and discrete goals. The completion of each step is a victory, a success. From the outside, Lucas may have looked like he was failing, but within his own experience, every completed step in his plan was a small victory, building confidence and skill that ultimately won his role in *High School Musical*.

SUCCESS REWARDS REPETITION

Excellence abides no shortcuts. One must do the work, and do it again and again, inching closer to the goal over time. Lucas perfected his callbacks by auditioning time and again before landing his first role, just like every young professional and seasoned veteran discussed in this book: Each one has perfected technique with repetition.

Consider an observation from a recent class meeting at SCAD—ILLU 309 Illustrating Beyond the Page: The Narrative Experience. The professor asked each student to generate a single visual idea:

a frog dancing with a bird, a child riding a gryphon, windblown dunes stretching to the horizon, and so on. Next, students were asked to create a thumbnail for the visual idea (i.e., a loose, quick sketch of an idea with minimal shading that helps artists select the ideal composition). The professor gave students five minutes, then each one stood and showed their thumbnail. Most were proud of their quick work.

"Okay," she said. "Now create a few more."

"How many?" one student asked.

"Fifty," she said.

The gasps were audible. Fifty's a lot of drawings, even if they're tiny.

In the next class, the professor then asked the students to narrow down their 50 thumbnails to the three strongest, resulting in a clear favorite for each student concept. In comparing the final/best thumbnail to the original, of which everyone had been so proud, the differences were obvious and vast. The repetition, it turned out, had not been repetition at all, but rather a gradual evolution into greater complexity. The more the students drew, the more refined their work became, until they discovered the perfect visual composition, which in almost all cases was the very last thumbnail. This, of course, doesn't mean those other 49 thumbnails were failures. Absolutely not. They were necessary stepping stones to success.

Whatever your professional goals, set aside time and create multiple iterations of the same idea (for example, a hashtag for a new campaign, or a narrative outline for a client pitch). Go the extra mile and create 20 or 30 ideas, stated in short form. This daily habit of the hands creates a kind of wondrous alchemy, allowing space for the mind to work, for concepts to evolve and skills to improve.

SUCCESS REWARDS HOPE

SCAD has had the privilege of hosting some of the world's greatest talents, winners of MacArthur Genius Grants, Presidential Medals of Freedom, Pulitzer Prizes, Pritzker Prizes, Woolmark Prizes, Tony Awards, Oscars, Emmys, Grammys, as well as celebrated CEOs and leaders in international business. You notice a few things about the most accomplished persons: They are kind, curious, and most importantly, brimming with genuine optimism. You don't climb to the very heights of Maslow's hierarchy without a belief that achieving success is possible.

One of our students' favorite designers and most admired entrepreneurs, Cynthia Rowley, attributes her success to what she calls "pathological optimism."

"I don't think about what's not working," she said in a recent On Creativity episode. "I address it and move on."

Her mantra is, "Deny, defy, sugarcoat."

Genuine optimism is not, as doubters suggest, naïve. Optimism forms the very root of resilience, and study after study shows how resilience and positive thinking are stronger predictors of success than I.Q.![55] Time and again, we see that the most successful people are those who manifest the highest levels of grit, rising up again and again to seize their goals. Optimists, according to psychologist Barbara Frederickson, are those who view tasks as challenges, a chance to prove themselves.[56]

"Having a positive outlook in difficult circumstances not only is an important predictor of resilience—how quickly people recover from adversity—but it is the most important predictor of it," writes Emily Smith in *The Atlantic*.[57]

EVERY DAY AFFORDS AN OPPORTUNITY

Lucas Grabeel has visited SCAD on several occasions, delivering master classes at SCAD aTVfest and SCAD AnimationFest in Atlanta. Recently, he addressed a room packed with imminent creative professionals—future animators, filmmakers, actors—and his words apply to any student in every vocation under the sun: "No matter what you do, you wake up every day and you create. That's your job. And yes, you need to know how to network and meet people and all that, but your focus must be on creating and bettering yourself and your skill every single day," Lucas said. "Your job is to create and the rest will fall into place. It might take five minutes. It might take five years, but if you persist and you keep creating and improving, you'll get there."

Keep your grandest goals in mind, yes, but focus on what's right in front of you: the day, the task, the moment. Instead of pining away, dreaming of what it's like to work at Samsung or Intel, spend the day searching for universities whose graduates go to work every day at these companies. Instead of fantasizing about how you'd be perfect at voicing the next DreamWorks or Pixar hero, buy the Blue Snowball microphone and make your own vocal demo. By week's end, you'll be that much closer to infinity and beyond.

Incremental success teaches you that dreams are achievable. You'll get a taste for triumph. You'll feel genuine pride, even from small victories. That memory of success helps create your next win. As the work of operations management researcher Bradley Staats has shown, we always learn and grow more when we succeed. Failure is not what it's cracked up to be.[58]

In the 1970s, right around the time SCAD was founded, Failure-ism had just become en vogue. Freeform, do-your-own-thing experimentation was all the rage. Rules went out the window. An emphasis on grammar and composition was replaced by an emphasis on stream-of-consciousness writing. In visual art, chance and happenstance ruled the day. The word "try" was tres chic, as though trying were enough. Failure was hot, back then.

At SCAD, we like to implement a different approach: Instead of celebrating failure, we struck the very word from our vocabulary, along with can't, won't, n'er, zilch, and nunca. Words are powerful. Our focus is wholly on the positive, and we live that ethos in every classroom and studio. On the first day of class each academic term, many of our professors like to remind the students that, according to the gradebook, everybody has a perfect grade. When it happens, eyes light up. Success, even the barest inkling of it, feels grand. Each day presents a perfect new opportunity to triumph.

Your journey lasts a lifetime, and every day should feel as hopeful and full of promise as the first day of school, when the whiteboards are clean, the pencils sharp, the notebooks ready and waiting, the gradebook pristine. Success doesn't have to be a mystery, and it doesn't have to be a buzzword. Success is intentional, an ethos, a way of life, a worldview that transforms talented, hardworking students into empowered, determined leaders.

Right now, in this very moment, you possess all the strength and determination necessary within yourself to press forward and rise to every occasion, win every contest, master every technique, succeed in any quest. Apply these seven lessons to the goodness you hold within your very own heart and prepare to ascend to the stars.

MAGNIFY THE

GOOD

~ GABRIEL GARCÍA MÁRQUEZ
author of One Hundred Years of Solitude

TO CHANGE THE WORLD

The one quality that unites every dreamer and maker across the planet is the gift of hope. The life of invention is a life of building better tomorrows, and if you've made it this far in our journey together, then you surely hold that very same hope in your own heart, too. You want to change the world! Don't you want to make the world more beautiful, more productive, more equitable for all? We do, too.

This desire, to share your gifts and passions with others to improve their lives, takes the dreamer beyond Maslow's fifth stage of self-actualization to an oft-overlooked stage of human development: the stage of "self-transcendence," added by Maslow some 26 years after his original theory was published. This new final step in human development describes the season when a person becomes motivated by values that transcend personal achievement, such as the pursuit of knowledge to benefit the greater good, spiritual yearning, and service to others.[59]

What makes today's students so remarkable, compared to earlier generations, is that they recognize the unique interplay of self-actualization and self-transcendence, how one can integrate the passionate pursuit of a calling *with* the principled pursuit of service to others. Today's dreamers want to make the world better with their professions, not just in their free time. At SCAD, we've seen this change-the-world altruism flourishing in our classrooms and our graduates. After watching a close family member fight through a terminal illness, Moksha, from Mumbai, India, applied her education in graphic design and visual experience to create an app that allows health care providers to communicate directly with patients and their families. She now works for The Weather Company, an IBM business, helping save lives through improved data visualization. In the early days of the COVID-19 outbreak, Moksha utilized artificial intelligence to design a hyper-local interactive map of coronavirus cases across the world, allowing users to track cases within their own communities.

At SCADpro, animation and other digital media students recently partnered with a primary researcher on an NIH (National Institutes of Health) grant to create a virtual reality tool to help stroke victims learn to walk again, applying their knowledge of gaming and digital environments to the human body. Another group of digital media students at SCAD recently partnered with hospice and other health care professionals to ease the pain of terminally ill patients using VR technology, helping users to experience pleasurable, comforting, and joyfully exhilarating moments (like flying in a virtual hot-air balloon) without leaving hospice care. This is what we do at SCAD, marrying research and technology to creativity. To shine a light. To heal. To make whole again.

Angela, a UX designer, is now working at Lenovo, a multi-national technology company, where she researches trends to guide the company's design decisions and serves in Lenovo's Product Diversity Office, ensuring that products are inclusive for all.

Brian, an art director, has dedicated himself to making self-care more inclusive with Hello Good Lookin', a new brand of non-gendered, affordable self-care products that help every human feel their feelings.

Visual artist Le'Andra, winner of the $200,000 ArtPrize, had already earned a business degree before returning to university to earn a B.F.A. in photography and explore hard questions about contemporary life—about identity, struggle, and freedom—to give voice to the voiceless in society.

Mir inspired his hometown community when he became the first Pakistani to win an Academy Award (he's won three so far) for visual effects in *The Golden Compass* (2007), followed by more visual effects Oscars for *Life of Pi* (2012) and *Frozen* (2013). Mir has brought hope and inspiration to all those who leave their homes and travel across oceans and borders to pursue an education and a calling.

No two paths to professional and personal fulfillment are quite the same, but it's our hope that you can apply these seven lessons throughout the great adventure of your life, at home, at university, and beyond.

1. HOLD YOUR HAND HIGH

2. NEVER MISS A FIELD TRIP

3. CAST YOUR DREAM CREW

4. PICK YOUR PERFECT SEAT

5. DO THE HOMEWORK

6. BE THE UNICORN

7. TREAT EVERY DAY LIKE THE FIRST

As you consider this book's seven lessons, construct actionable intentions about how you can help make the world better while you also build your own future. For example, you hold your hand high (Lesson One) when you ask questions—and also when you volunteer to help others. And world changers absolutely need to make every field trip (Lesson Two) because you can't change the world if you don't see it first! To achieve your own self-actualization and self-transcendence, emulate the careers and choices of the heroes and rising stars described in this book.

Each of these professionals stood exactly where you stand today, looking toward the horizon, ready to commence their journeys. They didn't yet have all the answers, and neither do you. But you know much. You have a vision. Plan the path to your best life and work your plan. And when knowing what's next seems impossible, embrace the beauty of ambiguity. There's freedom in not needing to know all the answers, at least not right now, as long as you know what matters most: keeping faith with your heart's desires and climbing that great pyramid toward your own destiny, one hopeful breath, one bold step at a time.

ACKNOWLEDGEMENTS

Thank you to the SCAD alumni and the many SCAD writers, designers, subject matter experts, educators, and special contributors, and a very special thanks to SCAD chief operating officer and alumnus Glenn Wallace, who first envisioned the original concept for this book.

Tabish Ahmed (M.F.A., interactive design and game development, 2014)

Mir Zafar Ali (B.F.A., visual effects, 2015)

Christopher Beard (M.A., industrial design and design for sustainability, 2018)

Kyle Blackmon (B.F.A., accessory design and fashion, 2011)

Melinda Borysevicz (B.F.A., painting, 2011)

Danielle Boykin (B.F.A., interior design, 2017)

Sarah Butler (B.F.A., fashion and graphic design, 2012)

Stephen Dowling (B.A., visual communication, 2014)

Erik Dunshee (B.F.A., product design, 2001)

Jason English (B.F.A., computer art and illustration, 2002)

Ian Felton (B.F.A., industrial design, 2015)

T. Gaffney, SCAD executive director of creative services and publishing

Jack Geshel (B.F.A., photography, 2017)

Yunman Gu (M.A., design management and industrial design, 2016)

Alexandra Hossick (B.F.A., fibers and jewelry, 2012)

Eliza Hunter (B.F.A., fibers, 2017)

Joel Kashuba (M.F.A., product design, 2002)

Harrison Scott Key, Ph.D. (M.F.A., writing, 2013), SCAD executive dean

Brian Lamy (B.F.A., advertising, 2016)

Richard Langthorne (B.F.A., visual communication, 2013)

Le'Andra LeSeur (B.F.A., photography, 2014)

Brett Levine, Ph.D., SCAD executive researcher

Josh Lind (B.F.A., film and television, 2005)

Adriana Manrique (M.F.A., animation, 2015; B.F.A., animation illustration, 2010)

Angela Martin (B.F.A., user experience (UX) design, 2020)

Jennifer McCarn (M.F.A., graphic design, 2002), SCAD senior art director

Ciaran McGuigan (B.F.A., film and television, 2014)

Chris Miller, SCAD executive director of operations

Zhu Mo (M.F.A., animation and motion media design, 2016)

Michael Mullan (M.F.A., illustration, 2010)

Erin Muntzert (B.F.A., graphic design and photography, 2004)

Warren Neiger (B.F.A., industrial design and service design, 2014)

Paula O'Callaghan (M.F.A., interior design, 1997)

Harrison Pink (B.F.A., interactive design and game development, 2008)

Moksha Rao (M.F.A, graphic design and visual experience, 2019)

Christina Ripley (B.F.A., fashion marketing and management, 2016)

David Rivera (B.F.A., dramatic writing, 2016)

Christopher John Rogers (B.F.A., fashion, 2016)

Logann Rogers (B.A., visual communication, 2012)

Tom Rouine (B.F.A., industrial design, 2017)

Corrine Saylor (B.F.A., fashion and interior design, 2004)

Laura Silva (B.F.A., writing, 2016)

Tiffani Taylor (M.F.A., painting, 2020; M.A., art history, 2003)

Jordan Trinci-Lyne (B.F.A., advertising, 2016)

Alexandra Tyson (B.F.A., fashion, 2016)

Colin Tunstall (B.F.A., graphic design and photography, 2003)

Shannon Vanderhill (M.F.A., design management, 2017)

Glenn Wallace (B.F.A., interior design, 1995), SCAD chief operating officer

Paula Wallace, SCAD president and founder

Jordan Wannemacher (B.A., visual communication, 2012)

Kari Waters, SCAD project manager of books

NOTES

FOREWORD: UP WE GO!

1   The "UX" denotes user experience design, a profession that creates positive interactions between humans and objects (e.g., phones, apps, websites, physical spaces). UX designers apply knowledge from psychology, programming, storytelling, graphic design, research, business strategy, and more. SCAD offers a B.F.A. in UX design that we developed in collaboration with Google.

LESSON № 1: HOLD YOUR HAND HIGH.

2   SCAD operates on the quarter system, rather than semesters, as quarters (where class meetings are longer and more frequent, but the term is slightly shorter) are demonstrated to increase depth of learning as well as student enjoyment of subject matter.

3   For more on our in-house research and design consultancy, check out scad.edu/scadpro. Find more on Clayco and SCADpro at claycorp.com/hard-hat-redesign.

4   Gardner's theory of multiple intelligences posits that all students possess intellectual aptitude. At SCAD, we believe our task as educators is to discover and cultivate each learner's natural gifts and inclinations. As for conscientiousness (what some call resilience or grit), we hold to the truism that every person is capable of hard work, especially when it connects to their deepest passions.

5   von Stumm et al., 2011.

6   Kaufmann, 2017.

7   Kennedy, 2015.

8   Dias and Kahn, 2016.

9   Hicklin, 2017.

10   Litman, et al., 2005.

11   Horrigan, 2016.

12   ResearchGate, 2014.

LESSON № 2: NEVER MISS A FIELD TRIP.

13   Assante and Smith, 2016.

14   Arup, 2016.

15   Wells, 2017.

16   Global Coalition on Aging, 2015.

17   PTI, 2018. https://economictimes.indiatimes.com/magazines/panache/how-to-improve-brain-power-try-virtual-reality-for-a-sharper-mind/articleshow/64614096.cms?from=mdr.

18   Wu, 2016. https://www.forbes.com/sites/lesliewu/2019/12/26/how-virtual-travel-could-help-with-overtourism/#373ccce17bc1.

19   Ibid.

20   Jiachen Mo, GlobalEDGE, 2020. (https://globaledge.msu.edu/blog/post/56837/the-future-of-virtual-reality--virtual-travel).

21   Vedantam, 2018.

22   Godart, 2015.

23   Crossman and Clarke, 2010.

24   Dodgson, 2017.

25   De Klerk, 2017.

LESSON № 3: CAST YOUR DREAM CREW.

26   Murphy, 2019.

27   Zapata, 2016.

28   Do, et al., 2017.

29   Carrell, et al., 2011.

30   Cigna, 2018.

31   Bethune, 2019.

32   Savoie, 2019.

33   Ibid.

LESSON № 4: PICK YOUR PERFECT SEAT.

34   Fitzsimmons, 2020.

35   Lederman, 2017.

36   Bui and Miller, 2017.

37   Selingo, 2017.

38   Rose, 2019.

LESSON № 5: DO THE HOMEWORK.

39   A 2019 study of recent SCAD graduates found that 99% of alumni were employed, pursuing further education, or both within 10 months of graduation, with 92% of those alumni employed in a creative discipline. For more information on the employment of our graduates, Google "SCAD employment study."

40   Chappelow, 2019.

41   Kalaichandran, 2017.

42   Children's Hospital Association, 2018.

43   Vincent, 2018.

44   Beyond measuring immediate quality, accreditation can have long-term implications. Receipt of federal (and sometimes state) student loans is contingent upon enrollment at an accredited institution, and following graduation, licensing boards and employers often require candidates to furnish degrees from accredited programs.

45 NCES, 2019.

46 U.S. Department of Education data shows that the most recent national cohort of student loan borrowers has a default rate of 10.1%. The default rate for SCAD graduates is 5.5% for the same cohort. For more information, go to scad.edu/about/institutional-effectiveness/student-achievement-data.

LESSON № 6: BE THE UNICORN.

47 Barrett, 2013.

48 Pitt and Tepper, 2011.

49 Makridis, 2017.

50 Hemelt, 2009.

51 A few other facts about double majors from the Teagle study: At any given time, approximately 10–15% of undergraduate students are double majors; most double majors are decided in sophomore year; and universities with 100 or more degree programs and higher average SAT/ACT scores have more double majors.

LESSON № 7: TREAT EVERY DAY LIKE THE FIRST.

52 On Creativity, Ep. 7, Dec. 18, 2019.

53 Ottati, et.al., 2015.

54 Gottschalk, et al., 2014.

55 Quast, 2017.

56 Smith, 2013.

57 Ibid.

58 Snow, 2014.

EPILOGUE: TO CHANGE THE WORLD

59 Koltko-Rivera, 2006.

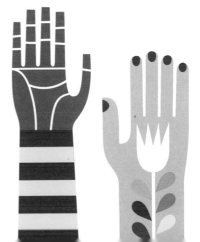

BIBLIOGRAPHY

Assante, CarylAnn, and Katie Smith. *Student and Youth Travel Digest: A Comprehensive Survey of the Student Travel Market*, 2016. https://www.syta.org/downloads/Student-and-Youth-Travel-Digest-Social-Impact-7.14.16.pdf.

Arup. *Cities Alive: Toward a Walking World*, 2016. https://www.arup.com/perspectives/publications/research/section/cities-alive-towards-a-walking-world.

Barrett, Dan. "Double Majors Produce Dynamic Thinkers, Study Finds." *The Chronicle of Higher Education*, March 15, 2013. https://www.chronicle.com/article/Double-Majors-Produce-Dynamic/137917.

Belli, "91 Percent of Teenagers Think They Know What Career They Want." *Payscale*, 2017. http://www.payscale.com/career-news/2017/07/teenager-career-choice-91-percent-teens-think-know-career-want.

Bethune, Sophie. "Gen Z More Likely to Report Mental Health Concerns." *Monitor on Psychology* 50 (1), 2019. https://www.apa.org/monitor/2019/01/gen-z.

Bui, Quoctrung, and Claire Cain Miller. "The Jobs You're Most Likely to Inherit From Your Mother and Father." *The New York Times*, November 22, 2017. https://www.nytimes.com/interactive/2017/11/22/upshot/the-jobs-youre-most-likely-to-inherit-from-your-mother-and-father.html.

Carrell, Scott E., Mark Hoekstra, and James E. West. 2011. "Is Poor Fitness Contagious? Evidence from Randomly Assigned Friends." *Journal of Public Economics* 95 (7/8): 657–63.

Chappelow, Jim. "Fundamental Analysis: Healthcare Sector." *Investopedia*, July 7, 2019. https://www.investopedia.com/terms/h/health_care_sector.asp.

Chiaet, Julianne. "Novel Finding: Reading Literary Fiction Improves Empathy." *Scientific American*, October 4, 2013. https://www.scientificamerican.com/article/novel-finding-reading-literary-fiction-improves-empathy.

Children's Hospital Association. "Virtual Reality Helps Reduce Patient Anxiety During Clinical Interventions." *Children's Hospital Association*, 2018. https://www.childrenshospitals.org/newsroom/childrens-hospitals-today/articles/2018/08/virtual-reality-helps-reduce-patient-anxiety-during-clinical-interventions.

Cigna. 2018. *U.S. Loneliness Index.*

Crossman, Joanna, and Marilyn Clarke. "International Experience and Graduate Employability: Stakeholder Perceptions on the Connection." *Higher Education* 59 (5), 2010: 599–613.

Dias, Marley, and Mattie Kahn. "Ballet Saved Misty Copeland From Middle School Misery." *ELLE*, September 9, 2016. https://www.elle.com/culture/interviews/a39099/misty-copeland-marley-mag-interview.

De Klerk, Amy. "Will Travelling the World Make You More Employable?" *Harper's Bazaar*, June 21, 2017. https://www.harpersbazaar.com/uk/travel/news/a42234/does-travelling-make-you-more-employable.

Djilic, Maja, Keith Oatley and Mihnea C. Moldoveanu. "Opening the Closed Mind: The Effect of Exposure to Literature on the Need for Closure." *Creativity Research Journal*, 25:2, 149-154, DOI: 10.1080/10400419.2013.783735.

Do, Kathy T., João F. Guassi Moreira, and Eva H. Telzer. "But Is Helping You Worth the Risk? Defining Prosocial Risk Taking in Adolescence." *Developmental Cognitive Neuroscience* 25, 2017: 260–71.

Dodgson, Lindsay. 2017. "More than 80% of Employers Think You're Better Suited for a Job If You've Been Travelling." *Business Insider*, June 16, 2017. https://www.businessinsider.com/travelling-make-you-more-employable-2017-6.

Fitzsimmons, Emma G. "Which Subway Seat Is Best? Your Answer Is Obviously Wrong." *The New York Times*, January 2, 2020. https://www.nytimes.com/2020/01/02/nyregion/best-subway-seat.html.

Global Coalition on Aging. "Destination Healthy Aging: The Physical, Cognitive, and Social Benefits of Travel," 2015. https://globalcoalitiononaging.com/wp-content/uploads/2018/07/destination-healthy-aging-white-paper_final-web.pdf.

Godart, Frédéric C., William W. Maddux, Andrew V. Shipilov and Adam D. Galinsky. "Fashion with a Foreign Flair: Professional Experiences Abroad Facilitate the

Creative Innovations of Organizations." *Academy of Management Journal* 58 (1). Published online 8 May 2014. https://journals.aom.org/doi/10.5465/amj.2012.0575.

Gottschalk, Sandra; Greene, Francis J.; Höwer, Daniel; Müller, Bettina. If you don't succeed, should you try again? The role of entrepreneurial experience in venture survival, *ZEW Discussion Papers*, No. 14-009, 2014. http://nbn-resolving.de/urn:nbn:de:bsz:180-madoc-358758.

Hemelt, Steven. "The college double major and subsequent earnings." October 9, 2009. https://www.tandfonline.com/doi/full/10.1080/09645290802469931?scroll=top&needAccess=true.

Hicklin, Aaron. "Misty Copeland: Dancing Into History." *The Guardian*, March 5, 2017. https://www.theguardian.com/stage/2017/mar/05/misty-copeland-principal-american-ballet-theatre-life-in-motion.

Horrigan, John. Lifelong Learning and Technology: Full Report. *Pew Research Center: Internet, Science & Tech*, 2016. https://www.pewresearch.org/internet/2016/03/22/lifelong-learning-and-technology-methodology.

Jacobs, Tom. "The Appeal of Ambiguity in Art." *The Week*, April 19, 2015. https://theweek.com/articles/548176/appeal-ambiguity-art.

Kalaichandran, Amelia. "Design Thinking for Doctors and Nurses." *The New York Times*, August 3, 2017. https://www.nytimes.com/2017/08/03/well/live/design-thinking-for-doctors-and-nurses.html.

Kaufmann, Scott Barry. "Schools Are Missing What Matters About Learning." *The Atlantic*, July 14, 2017. https://www.theatlantic.com/education/archive/2017/07/the-underrated-gift-of-curiosity/534573.

Kennedy, James. "High-Achieving Students Ask For More Help." *James Kennedy*, June 1, 2015. https://jameskennedymonash.wordpress.com/2015/06/01/high-achieving-students-ask-for-more-help.

Koltko-Rivera, Mark. "Rediscovering the Later Version of Maslow's Hierarchy of Needs: Self-Transcendence and Opportunities for Theory, Research, and Unification." American Psychological Association, December 12, 2005. https://www.researchgate.net/profile/Mark_Koltko-Rivera.

Lahiri, Jhumpa. *The Notebook*, 2003.

Lederman, Doug. "Who Changes Majors? (Not Who You Think)." *Inside Higher Ed*, December 8, 2017. https://www.insidehighered.com/news/2017/12/08/nearly-third-students-change-major-within-three-years-math-majors-most.

Litman, Jordan, Tiffany Hutchins, and Ryan Russon. "Epistemic Curiosity, Feeling-of-Knowing, and Exploratory Behaviour." *Cognition & Emotion* 19 (4), 2005: 559-582. doi:10.1080/02699930441000427.

Makridis, Christos. "Does It Pay to Get a Double Major?" *Quartz*. March 30, 2017. https://qz.com/945083/new-research-suggests-it-really-does-pay-to-get-a-double-major-in-college.

Marcellus, Sibille. "Here's How Workers Are Using Side Hustles to Get Ahead." *Yahoo Finance*, June 5, 2019. https://finance.yahoo.com/news/heres-how-workers-are-using-side-hustles-to-get-ahead-112347456.html.

Modak, Sebastian. "Travel." *New York Times Review of Books*, May 20, 2020. https://www.nytimes.com/interactive/2020/books/summer-reading.html.

Murphy, Melinda. "Dream Jobs: Meet a Luxury Resort Designer." *PressReader*, Nov. 1, 2019. https://www.pressreader.com/singapore/expat-living-singapore/20191101/281582357454646.

The National Center for Education Statistics. 2019. "Undergraduate Retention and Graduation Rates." https://nces.ed.gov/programs/coe/indicator_ctr.asp.

Ottati, Victor, Erika Price, Chase Wilson, and Nathanael Sumaktoyo. "When Self-Perceptions of Expertise Increase Closed-Minded Cognition: The Earned Dogmatism Effect." *Journal of Experimental Social Psychology* 61, 2015: 131–38.

Pitt, Richard, and Stephen Tepper. "Double Majors: Influences, Identities, and Impacts." *Teagle Foundation*, 2011. https://www.researchgate.net/publication/279985369_Double_Majors_Influences_Identities_and_Impacts.

Quast, Lisa. "Why Grit Is More Important Than IQ When You're Trying To Become Successful." *Forbes*, March 6, 2017. https://www.forbes.com/sites/lisaquast/2017/03/06/why-grit-is-more-important-than-iq-when-youre-trying-to-become-successful/#1e054c0a7e45.

ResearchGate. "Doing Good and Feeling Well: Exploring the Relationships Between Charitable Activities and Perceived Personal Wellness," 2013. http://www.researchgate.net/publication/257672500_Doing_Good_and_Feeling_Well_Exploring_the_Relationship_Between_Charitable_Activity_and_Perceived_Personal_Wellness.

Rose, Lacey. "How Reese Witherspoon Took Charge of Her Career and Changed Hollywood." *The Hollywood Reporter*, December 11, 2019. https://www.hollywoodreporter.com/features/how-reese-witherspoon-took-charge-her-career-changed-hollywood-1260203.

Savoie, Gabrielle. "This New Design Duo Is Making Velvet Furniture in Candy Colors." *Domino*, June 28, 2019. https://www.domino.com/content/orior-furniture.

Selingo, Jeffrey. "Six Myths About Choosing a College Major." *The New York Times*, November 3, 2017. https://www.nytimes.com/2017/11/03/education/edlife/choosing-a-college-major.html.

Sloan, Jordan Taylor. "Science Shows How Piano Players' Brains Are Actually Different From Everybody Else's." *Mic*, June 20, 2014. https://www.mic.com/articles/91329/science-shows-how-piano-players-brains-are-actually-different-from-everybody-elses#.G9ArNm5ma.

Smith, Emily Esfahani. "The Benefits of Optimism Are Real." *The Atlantic*, March 1, 2013. https://www.theatlantic.com/health/archive/2013/03/the-benefits-of-optimism-are-real/273306.

Snow, Shane. "Silicon Valley's Obsession With Failure Is Totally Misguided." *Business Insider*, October 13, 2014. https://www.businessinsider.com/startup-failure-does-not-lead-to-success-2014-10.

Vedatam, Shankar. "The Edge Effect." *Hidden Brain*. July 2, 2018. https://www.npr.org/transcripts/625426015?storyId=625426015?storyId=625426015.

Vincent, James. "Haptic Feedback Is Making VR Surgery Feel Like the Real Thing." *The Verge*, August 14, 2018. https://www.theverge.com/2018/8/14/17670304/virtual-reality-surgery-training-haptic-feedback-fundamentalvr.

von Stumm, Sophie, Benedikt Hell, and Tomas Chamorro-Premuzic. "The Hungry Mind: Intellectual Curiosity Is the Third Pillar of Academic Performance." *Perspectives on Psychological Science* 6 (6), 2011: 574-588. doi:10.1177/1745691611421204.

Wells, Katie. "Ecotherapy: The Health Benefits of Nature." *Wellness Mama*, October 7, 2019. https://wellnessmama.com/56086/nature-health-benefits.

YouthTruth. "Learning from Student Voice: College and Career Readiness," 2016. http://youthtruthsurvey.org/wp-content/uploads/2016/01/YouthTruth-Learning-From-Student-Voice-College-and-Career-Readiness-2016.pdf.

Zapata, Maria. "Senior Collections: Christopher John Rogers." The Manor, 2016. https://scadmanor.com/senior-collections-christopher-john-rogers.

SKY'S THE LIMIT!

SCAD: THE UNIVERSITY FOR CREATIVE CAREERS

The Savannah College of Art and Design is a private, nonprofit, accredited university, offering more than 100 academic degree programs in more than 40 majors across its locations in Atlanta and Savannah, Georgia; Lacoste, France; and online via SCAD eLearning.

SCAD enrolls approximately 15,000 undergraduate and graduate students from more than 100 countries. The innovative SCAD curriculum is enhanced by advanced professional-level technology, equipment, and learning resources, as well as opportunities for internships, professional certifications, and collaborative projects with corporate partners. In 2019, the prestigious Red Dot Design Rankings placed SCAD as the No. 1 university in the U.S. and in the top two universities in the Americas and Europe for the third consecutive year. Career preparation is woven into every fiber of the university, resulting in a superior alumni employment rate. In a study of Spring 2019 SCAD graduates, 99% were employed, pursuing further education, or both within 10 months of graduation.